Seven Wagons and a Half

Basque Originals Series No. 22

Seven Wagons and a Half
Growing Up Basque Didn't Hurt
By
Jim Barayasarra

Center for Basque Studies
University of Nevada, Reno
2019

Dedication

To
Nemesio Barayasarra and Maria Carmen Solay,
my proud Basque immigrant parents,

and
Marian Janet Anchustegui
my proud Basque wife and all immigrants to America.

Acknowledgements

Eskerrik asko

To the Center for Basque Studies at the University of Nevada, Reno for choosing my book for publication under the direction of Xabier Irujo, and also to Daniel Montero, who suggested the 2019 Writing Contest. Also, of course, to Cameron Watson, Carly Sauvageau, and Meggan Laxalt Mackey for excellent editing.

Eskerrik asko

To Shirley Thompson, my creative writing teacher, who gave me the guidance and confidence to write. Also to Louise K. Cadby, former stage and screen actress, who shared my early writings with her professional friends whose comments were an inspiration to me.

Eskerrik asko

To the following who have been sources of help and encouragement: Margaret Tessier, Jim Chance, Doug Besser, and Jeannie Parker. The list includes Tom Boyle, a recently naturalized citizen, Martin Jenkins, who became like a son to me, David Hoxie, who has a story to tell, Steve Canaday, whom I have challenged to make me like Shakespeare because I know he can, and Rosita Skoro for advice, Deborah Camp for excellent illustrations, my writing group (especially Frances Mason), and finally Joe Louis, a hero of Nemesio and me.

Eskerrik asko

Of course, to my family: my wife, Jan, and my children—Latif, Christina, Lisa, and Mary whose help, patience, and love far exceed any comments I could make here.

Eskerrik asko

To all those not listed here who were such inspirations to me.

Seven Wagons and a Half
Basque Originals Series No. 22
Center for Basque Studies
University of Nevada, Reno
1664 North Virginia St.
Reno NV 89577-2322 USA
http://basque.unr.edu

.

Library of Congress Cataloging-in-Publication Data

Names: Barayasarra, James, author.
Title: Seven wagons and a half : growing up Basque didn't hurt / by James
Barayasarra.
Description: Reno : Center for Basque Studies, 2020. | Series: Basque
original series ; no. 22
Identifiers: LCCN 2020010914 | ISBN 9781949805208 (paperback)
Subjects: LCSH: Barayasarra, James. | Barayasarra, James--Family. | Basque
Americans--Idaho--Anecdotes.
Classification: LCC E184.B15 B36 2020 | DDC 305.899/920796--dc23
LC record available at https://lccn.loc.gov/2020010914

CONTENTS

Introduction

I first called my efforts *American Candy* but learned that candy has a special meaning—"Eye Candy" to some refers to *good-looking men*. That is not what I write about so I chose another Basque expression, *Zazpi Gurdi eta Erdi*, which means Seven Wagons and a Half, a better topic in that it was not confused with "Eye Candy."

I kept "America's Candy" as the title of one episode because of the good stuff in America—the jobs, the opportunities, the freedom. And Mom often said/sang a little verse, "Fine and Dandy. American Candy. California Brandy."

Zazpi Gurdi eta Erdi, or *Seven Wagons and a Half*, also lends itself to important symbolic comparisons. There are seven Basque provinces in Spain and France and there are many Basques in America—again, which could be thought of as the eighth grouping or province, the half wagon, so to speak.

I see the same symbolism in the Nemesio's and Victorina's immigrant family—there were seven second generation children. Felipa had Victorina Marie, who, because of Felipa's divorce, was raised as a member of the same family, so again, beyond the seven and like one half wagon.

I wrote my stories pretty much as independent episodes and not in exact chronological order. Some stories are related and they are grouped together as parts. I tried different styles and at times I used personal pronouns and at other times I used Jimmy. Sometimes he was "Dad" but usually he was Nemesio. Very seldom as Frank. I had in mind the stories occurring as answers to a child saying "Tell us about the time you..."

Sometimes my language was rough but that was the way it was. At times, we seem to be superstitious (the owl). At times, at least two siblings thought I was being disrespectful to dad (breeding the cow). Lou said, "We don't want to embarrass the family." He shared very little with me. Felipa was the best source other than my own memory. Some names have been changed to not embarrass anyone.

All the episodes are based on true events. Of course, conversations are what I imagined them to be. I tried to be as close to what the real person was or would say.

The language is rough in many episodes but for these people with minimal schooling, in many cases, that was the norm. It was not uncommon to find someone who could swear the bucket full and yet be the kindest, the most generous and most loving Christian.

As part of my introduction, I call your attention to two episodes, "As a Matter of Fact," in which language competence or lack of it can lead to misunderstandings. In this episode, it all ended okay. But even in this episode, the lady's feelings were hurt.

The second, "*Kakaleku baxu deku zu,*" ("Your ass-hole is too low") points out a cultural difference, and I lived through this difference. In my American culture, such as in school, using the words "ass-hole" was not acceptable and in the Basque portion "*kakaleku*" was acceptable.

An example of cultural differences clashing: A Basque sheepherder was introduced to a very pregnant American lady. He patted her stomach and said, with a smile, "Hmm, pretty soon, you have puppies!" To him the remark was not offensive but she found it crude and out of line.

My last story is an attempt to show that although I am the only living person from my parent's first and second generation around, the story goes on. The story is there. I tried to picture how rough immigrant life was. And it kept on going: That seventeen-year-old had it tough but he kept going. That beautiful saint who was my mother, who wore out her husband's shoes had to hide her own wellbeing but she kept on going. We were poor but goddam it we kept on going. The best thing I inherited from my parents was their poverty. I wouldn't trade that poverty for all the riches in the world—not even the cardboard box in the middle of a dirt road in Grand View, Idaho would I trade. I was there before Grand View got its first telephone, upstairs above the Square Deal Store.

Am I a saint? Hell no, not even close, although I worry that I have not given to the least of my brothers, or even bought a brother a cold Budweiser at 3:00 p.m., when he worked all day in a hay field. I hope to hear "I was hot and thirsty and you gave me a cold bud."

My feelers are out now.

Episode 1

As a Matter of Fact

Mother is Fat

"As a matter of fact, that is cor ..." One of us would get interrupted.

"That is enough of that." Mom would say as she passed through the room with an arm load of laundry, "I could use a little help about now."

"Sure what do you need?"

"What do I need? WHAT–DO–I–NEED? What does it look like I am doing?"

"Carrying clothes to the washing machine. Are there more?"

"Just seven wagons and a half more. *Jesus, Maria, eta Jose*. And Mother is fat!"

As we returned to our homework, "Did you hear what she said?"

"*Jesus, Maria, eta Jose*?"

"No, she always says that—she said 'As a matter of fact!'"

"No? Did she?"

"As a matter of fact she ..."

"Again, Again? I KNOW MOTHER IS FAT. But is that all you have to talk about, Mother is VERY FAT?"

"Oh! We didn't say Mother is fat—we said as a matter of fact!"

"You didn't say Mother is fat—you said Mother is fat ..."

"No! No, No. Listen we did not say Mother is FAT. We said AS A MATTER OF FACT. Two different words. *Mother* and *matter* and *fat* and *fact*." After several repeats, finally ending in hugs and tears of joy.

This incident will be my introduction. As a second generation American, I lived in two cultures, one at school and a different one at home. My parents had minimal formal education but they were intelligent and were self-taught. As the sole survivor of their family, I must tell their story as a matter of fact.

Episode 2
Kakaleku baxu deku zu

"*Kakaleku baxu deku zu.*" "Your asshole is too low." That's what she'll say. Every time I want something—and she can't come up with one decent, not even one decent reason—I shouldn't have it, she resorts to that same old line. I've heard it a million times;

"Your *kakaleku* is too low." Why can't she be like normal moms? I can't go back to my friends and tell them, "I can't go to the picture show with you because my mother says that my asshole is too low." Good God, Almighty, they already think I'm weird when I speak that foreign stuff to her.

All I need to do is repeat that one pet saying of hers and I'll be the laughing stock of Grand View, Idaho, United States of America. I'd just as well enter the nut house, or join the French Foreign Legion, or become a priest in some far away land where they eat people. Maybe I should just do that or at least run away and then she will have time to think about my *kakaleku*—that it was not too high or too low—that I had a just-right *kakaleku* all along. She just doesn't understand. She is so old and doesn't let me do anything

"*Bai*, of course."

"But Mama, all the other—WHAT?"

"*Bai.* Yes. Hurry, your friends are waiting. And here is an extra dime for a bottle of pop afterwards."

"*Eskerrik asko.* Thank you, Mama. You are the best Mama in the whole world. Your *kakaleku* is just right."

Episode 3

Introduction: Continued

My last story, "I Can Pick Out my Own Bananas: The Unfinished Musical," takes a peek at a couple of old people, my oldest brother, Louie, and my sister, Felipa, but that's alright as I am now older than they were. I see an excellent musical with title song called "I Can Pick Out My Own Bananas; I Can Pick Out My Own." Can't you see the entire store produce people joining in a big chorus line carrying my sister on their shoulders? I give you permission to steal my idea.

Break a leg.

Eskerrik asko!

Episode 4

America's Candy

"Fine and dandy, America's candy, California brandy."

Sheepherders were often paid once or twice a year. Any other time involved asking the foreman for a "draw" or advance on wages due. Room and board were provided as part of the pay; and although not especially an attractive offer for Americans, it was enough to attract the Basque male to the United States. The American citizen was not equipped for the extremely long periods of isolation and loneliness which faced the herder—sometimes going weeks or longer without seeing another human.

Nemesio Barayasarra was such a herder, leaving Spain in 1914, to herd a band of sheep in southern Idaho. All of seventeen years of age, he said "goodbye" to parents and family and left for America where *everyone was rich, and hope, promises, and freedom beckoned the poor, discouraged, and oppressed*—not that he felt at all oppressed.

"I will, I'll take care of myself."

"I know—but you're my baby. It was just yesterday I brought you into this world."

"I have to go. There are no jobs here. After a couple of years, I will return. I promise. I promise." He hugged and kissed his mother, both in tears. With the corner of her apron she wiped away her tears and then his, as if somehow this amounted to lighting a candle. While his words to his mother were positive and promising, his inner feelings were not quite as confident.

That day, Candido, his father, hugged his son for the first and last time in the boy's life. Nemesio left the family, hurried to board the swine freighter which would get him to New York, America. His job was to care for the hogs, making sure they were properly fed and cared for. The grunting of the hogs, as they fought over the food, replaced his mother's singing while the stench of their bowels replaced the smell of homemade bread. Was he doing the right thing?

He arrived in New York City and was eventually taken to Ellis Island, where he and others were processed one by one. The authorities checked papers, looked for lice, asked questions, and eventually authorized Nemesio to enter to work with sheep.

He sat there on that wooden bench at Ellis Island wearing the "dress" trousers he saved for that day, his homemade cardboard suitcase at his side, and a small bundle of laundry smelling of pigs.

They all had peculiar odors about them—odor of musty clothes, odor of spicy food and garlic, and odors of pigs. Immigration officers, from time to time, would complain, "They stink!" They always spoke loudly to him.

Nemesio followed advice given to him by others, answered questions and followed directions without question, wasn't a wise ass, and said "Thank you, Sir" over and over again. "Red Hairs" (the name Basques called Americans among themselves). He followed the advice given to the letter even though a couple of times he wanted to call them "Sons of Bitches." He, Juan, and a German made it through and thanked God. They included prayers for the Chinaman who didn't.

The next day he hurried to board the train for Mountain Home, Idaho and the Plaza Ranch. That night he crawled into his sleeping birth and as he thought of his mother and Spain, he cried himself to sleep.

Episode 5

A Day in the Life of a Lonely Sheepherder

A coyote howl from the East was answered in kind from the West. The thousand or so sheep huddled in the moonlit night with a few along the periphery getting up and moving toward the center of the band, nervous from the coyotes' howls.

Patxi (pronounced pa-chee), a border collie, lay at Nemesio's feet, occasionally getting up to survey the sheep. If any were beginning to wander, Patxi would slink to the wayward lamb, nip at its heels, and chase it back to the band. Although trained by the herder, a dog instinctively knows some of the basics and bonds with the herder as a child bonds with his mother. As the sun sank, Nemesio and Patxi sat on the tongue of the wagon as part of an evening ritual with them. "You sit there as I talk to you. What do you care, you crazy Kokolo? As long as I toss you a bone now and then you're happy! And they say a dog has a hard life—if only..." He didn't finish as he thought of Spain and his mother.

The dog moved closer to Nemesio's leg for that rewarding pat on the head as the young herder continued, "Yes Patxi, at least I have you. These days and nights are lonely enough even with you to talk to. I can't read English yet. I've read these few Spanish books to death and you don't seem to have much to say, right?" He returned to his silence, as tears welled up in his eyes and ran down his cheeks, until one of his mother's tunes entered his thought. "Well, time to hit the sack. You watch the sheep, boy. Let me know if those coyotes get any closer." He took the lantern and stepped onto the tongue to enter his summer palace, half singing, half crying.

The inside of the palace was a six foot by eight foot camp wagon with a sleeping bunk across the back, a small two foot by two foot table and a wood burning stove in front. His coffee sat on the back burner while the front burner was used to cook on, heat water, and whatever it was needed for. Clothes were either stacked under the bunk or piled on the floor.

Although tired, sleep did not come right away as Nemesio thought over the events of the day, about tomorrow when he would move the band to the meadow by the lake. The sheep could graze in that area for the next three or four days. He would be on guard for coyotes. They were especially bad this year—as they always were every four years, the year after the jackrabbit population peaked then mysteriously disappeared. Wondering why that was, his eyes began to close.

Then he thought of Spain, his family, and how they all were. Oh, how much he missed them. Tomorrow he would write them a long letter: "I will! I will! God, don't let me forget." The coyote medley provided an eerie background for the restless dream-filled night.

Patxi was in charge.

Episode 6

Another Hole in the Pants

"Agur zaharra makakue."
Nemesio

It was another evening at the camp wagon for Nemesio, Patxi, and the sheep. He shot two coyotes that day and placed the dead animals on poles at opposite ends of the band as if the ritual would warn other coyotes that the same was in store for them. Earlier he placed poison in the sheep carcasses the coyotes had killed the night before, placing the poison in an uneaten, untouched part of the sheep. He was told that coyotes tend to open a new area to be eaten never eating from the same wound.

He felt uneasy about something—of what he wasn't sure. Something about that "Red Hair" on horseback he encountered earlier was just not right. What was he doing here? The closest house was fifteen miles away—across the mountain.

"God damn, Red Hair," he would say to Patxi, "I don't trust him, not one goddamn bit. That son of a bitch had to be up to something.

"Robinson's Cattle Ranch did hire twenty, twenty-five cowboys on their spread some thirty miles away, across the mountain. Last year, if it weren't for that kid they hired who came early to warn me, I—"

His half thoughts/half conversation could not continue when he realized he would have died. Then, as if a revelation hit him, "The cowboy—earlier—maybe a warning." *Zzz-innng!*

"That was a shot! Couldn't have been six inches from my ear!"

Nemesio took cover under the wagon. His eyes surveyed the horizon. Nothing. Finally, after what seemed an eternity, he instructed the dog,

"Well, Patxi, I can't stay under here forever. If he shoots me, he shoots me! If he does, Patxi, you go out and bite his balls!"

He crawled out, stood up and yelled, "Come on, you son of a bitch, shoot. Shoot me, *cabrón!*" But no shots came. This had happened before and it was starting again.

He went into the camp wagon to fix pancakes for supper and relax. It was easier in daylight. He opened a can of evaporated milk and went to the flour sack with a cup. "Did that sack move? God. Oh, God. I am losing my mind." He thrust his hand in as he heard a familiar whirr, just before he felt the snake strike his sleeve. The snake's fangs were caught in the cuff of his faded plaid work shirt. He grabbed the snake with his other hand and flipped it out the door "Thank you, God," and then to no one in particular, "probably had it senses dulled by the flour."

"How the hell can one take these things? Goddamn Red Hair! No way that rattler got into that sack on its own."

The pounding of his heart complemented the mournful song of the coyotes as he examined every inch of the camp wagon and decided that from then on, he would stretch a thin thread across the opening of the wagon. Anyone entering would not see the thread and break it. The incident was reported to the foreman the following week but not to the law, a Red Hair and a goddamn Ku Klux Klan member.

Exhausted, he fell asleep—not the restful sleep he needed and wanted but a sleep full of those incessant nightmares he had ever since he left the Pyrenees.

"Well. God. One more day! I made it through one more day. What will tomorrow bring? Probably another hole in the pants."

Episode 7
Sheepherder's Day on the Town
Part 1: Mouse Sundae

If the herders were paid a few times a year, it was during a slack period, such as after shipping when the fatted lambs were separated from the ewes and shipped to markets such as Ogden, Salt Lake, or Omaha. The herders used this time to buy whatever supplies were needed, or to send money home to families in Spain. This time was always one of pride, for each hoped to hear that his lambs were the heaviest. More often than not, Nemesio had the heaviest lambs and his pride would show through, although he didn't notice.

Separating the lambs for shipping was often followed by culling the ewes not fit enough for another season in the hills. Some of the better culled sheep made it to small farms which did not graze their animals on BLM (Bureau of Land Management) forest. The rest were sold to meat packers, probably used in canned soups.

During this off time, the herders stayed at boarding houses in Boise, Mountain Home, Shoshone, and other towns where herders gathered. Faustino ran such an establishment which served meals family style along with boot-legged whiskey. He employed several housekeeping people, including a lady, Juanna, who had a ravenous appetite for ice cream.

Faustino's place had two large adjoining rooms. The bar was in one room and the other room contained an upright piano at one end and card tables for *mus* and other card games occupying the rest of the space. If a talented boarder were present, he would play the piano joined by someone with spoons. Songs from Spain completed the nightly show.

One day when the herders had way, way too much to drink, they decided to play a trick on Juanna and that was to put a dead mouse in her ice cream. "I can't wait to see her find the mouse. Everyone is in on this together? Right?"

"Well, Carlos, if you need everyone's support to do it, just don't do it. Why you afraid to stand alone? Count me out!" Nemesio left to have a cigarette and do what he knew he had to.

"Wait, Juanna. I need to talk to you."

"Hello, Nemesio, how sweet of you to wait for me."

"Just don't eat any ice cream today. Please!" The pleading was as desperate as any issue in his young life.

"Why not, Nemesio?" she teased, "You don't want me to get fat?"

"Please, Juanna, just don't. I can't tell you why."

"Just you or any man try and stop me. Tell me or you be sorry."

"Alright, Juanna. Don't tell the men. They put a dead mouse in your ice cream. As a joke! I couldn't let that go."

"A mouse in my ice cream? A MOUSE IN MY ICE CREAM!"

"Okay! Shhh. Quiet. Don't tell anyone I told you."

"Thank you, Nemesio. I know who came up with the joke. I am going in with my opening number." The door opened and the spotlight shone on her. Thunderous applause greeted her as she entered the room. She stopped at her table and picked up her bowl of ice cream. She danced through the crowd using her scarves and ice cream as props. When she reached Carlos, she faked a stumble and dropped the ice cream upside down on his head.

"Who told you?" Carlos objected.

"I did!" said Nemesio. During the rest of the evening, the men all apologized to Juanna and then to Nemesio.

Postscript

I was born in Bengochea's Hotel in Mountain Home, Idaho. Why that location, I am not sure, other than at the time, I decided that "it ain't gonna get any better than this." I made my curtain call and I've never been the same since. I am honored since those before me and one after me were Grand View-ites. Frank was the biggest and last for Grand View so that Mike and Manuel happened in a hospital in Boise.

A couple of summers ago my family stopped there and the new owners at that time recorded my visit and gave me a tour. I saw where and how the bootleg whiskey was hidden in plain sight along the stairway—even knowing where it was, I could not tell it was there. I always suspected. I was famous. If they make a movie of me, Danny Devito will have to be me. Denzel Washington will be heartbroken.

Episode 7
Sheepherder's Day on the Town
Part 2: Six Bits—For Coffee?

At another time, Nemesio, having a few drinks with the boys, felt he had reached his limit. Since most of the crowd had already gone, he ordered a cup of coffee to top the evening off. His last two friends left as Nemesio asked, "What do I owe for the coffee?"

"Oh, I don't know," as he sized how drunk Nemesio was, "Six bits should be about right."

"Oh," Nemesio thought to himself as he tossed three quarters on the counter, "Okay but you will pay, Maleta." He made a restroom pit stop off the second overflow room. As expected, Chalie was dozing in the back of the room. Chalie, a Red Hair, hung around for free drinks but all the herders knew he was a snitch for the bartender. "Good," Nemesio thought as he climbed up on the piano bench, stood up, and unzipped his fly.

"What are you going to do, Nemesio?" Chalie took the bait.

"Pee in the piano, Chalie," he said, as Chalie left to tell. Then, Nemesio climbed down and left, with parting words over his shoulder, "Someday I'll let you know, I didn't pee in your goddamn piano but not until I get six bits *worth* of flesh."

Oh what a good day!

Episode 8

Courtship of Nemesio and Victorina

Nemesio was twenty-seven when he and Victorina were married. The eleven-year period he had spent in America taught him the bitter lesson that America was not the land of candy he dreamed of. Also, he was not able to visit the old country and the family he left there. He had known Victorina in Spain but since she was eight years younger than he and only nine years of age, no romantic interests existed. It was later, when she became an adult, and developed into a beautiful young lady, that he began writing to her. The suggestion that they write to each other probably came through their two mothers who were sisters. It was through this exchange of letters that they learned about each other and fell in love. Finally, a marriage proposal was made by Nemesio through the mail and accepted by Victorina, also through the mail.

This initiated a flurry of letters, concerning how this marriage would take place. Victorina could not come to America, since she was not a herder and coming as a normal tourist was much too expensive. It would be impossible for her to make the trip. It was felt that a trip to Spain by Nemesio was also out of the question, since that too would cost precious savings and cut further into survival earnings. The suggestion was made by a priest in Spain that the marriage could be conducted using proxies.

It was decided: a small family ceremony would take place in Bustudi, Victorina's home village in Spain with someone standing in for Nemesio, and a similar ceremony would take place in Idaho with a proxy for Victorina.

With the minimum number of family or friends as witnesses, and with the appropriate signatures, the marriage was completed on February 21, 1925. Maria Carmen Victorina Monasterio Solay became Maria Carmen Victorina Solay de Barayasarra, the wife of a legal United

States resident. She could now make the journey as a legal immigrant and booked passage on a ship with funds sent.

Newly married Victorina was accompanied by her three sisters and her father; Maria, Concha, Berta & Elojio. The sisters said goodbye in San Cristobal while Elojio continued on to Bordeaux, France where Victorina was to board the *Ile de France*. Elojio said his goodbyes and left to return home. She met seven other Basques and since the ship was delayed for eight hours, they did some local sightseeing. After arriving in America, and while Nemesio continued as a herder, Victorina was employed as a cook for the sheep company during lambing season, early February, when all the herders were in the winter camp. This was a very busy, yet interesting time for the herders since it was not as lonely, and allowed them to socialize with each other.

Nemesio and Victorina set up housekeeping in a tent during some of the early years of their marriage. An eighty-acre farm was purchased in Grand View, Idaho just before the stock market crash and the start of the Great Depression. This farm was to be the family's home through the Depression, the War Years, and into 1949 when the farm was sold and the family moved to a rented sixty acres in Nampa, Idaho. While living in Grand View, all the children were born to the couple, from Louis in 1929 to Manuel in 1944. Two children died during this time: Alva in 1934, at age two and Manuel in 1945, at age one and a half.

Each event made the "Candy" dream more elusive with new happenings testing the family's resolve even further. Each positive encouragement was always tempered with the reality and memory of hard times. The coming of a second Depression replaced the second coming of Christ as the dominating factor in their lives.

Barayasarra Nemesio
C/O Plaza Ranch
Mt. Home   Idaho.

Episode 9

A Poor Basco Buys a Farm

Was the American Dream falling into place? Or was it falling apart? The future was expected to continue much the same as the past. The Roaring Twenties were fun times—even bootleg whiskey was doing a brisk business and thriving quite well in the Basque boarding houses.

And Nemesio, now thirteen years older than the seventeen-year-old teen who left the old country, was able to adjust to life in America although much of it was not the friendliest toward a low-life Black Basco. Survival requires trust and trust may imply risk. Nemesio trusted Sam Mullinex and Fay and Gertrude Byfield—good choices. Now he had to adjust to a strange change again— married life to a semi-stranger.

Eventually, enough of a nest egg was accumulated that, with some help, Nemesio could buy the eighty-acre farm he found for sale. It wasn't much to look at, and certainly needed tons of work. For example, a ditch had to be dug to drain out the swamping area in the middle. The house had no plumbing of any kind and no heat other than the kitchen stove and an old potbelly stove in one bedroom. The fire in each stove would burn out sometime during the night. Many a cold winter night the bucket of drinking water that was always kept sitting by the stove was frozen solid by morning. Dad would get up before 4:00 a.m. every day to start the fires. The potbelly stove that heated the bedrooms was within sight of my bed, and I was entertained many mornings by peeking out from under the sheets and seeing Dad's bare ass on display through the gap in the back of his long-johns, as he bent over to start the fire.

Nemesio approached Benito, a wealthy Basque, to see if the needed loan could be negotiated. "Why, of course, Nemesio, I would be honored to finance your loan. A hard worker like you is just what that property needs to improve its value."

"Well, it looks like we have a deal." Nemesio said as he stretched his hand over the table to seal the contract, with the binding handshake. Hands shook but then . . .

"You do understand, the farm will be in my name until you get it paid off."

"No deal, Benito! If you can't trust me any more than that, I don't trust you either. If I give a man my word, even shake hands over it, I keep it. I expect the same in return."

Although Dad said very little, word spread so that a couple of visits resulted from other Basques with offers to loan him the funds. Dad rejected both, "about the same as the first, no deal then, no deal now."

Nemesio's friend, Felipe came to see him. Both men talked about everything and said nothing, dancing around the real issue du jour. As they walked to the car Felipe put his left hand on Nemesio's shoulder, and with his right hand grabbed Nemesio's right hand in a shaking manner and emotionally said, "I am loaning you what you need on YOUR terms. I've known you all my life, friend, and a more honest and hard-working person does not exist—a little bull-headed but otherwise fine."

"Well. . .er . . .I—"

"Nothing to say, friend! Just be wary of Benito, he's a coyote if ever one exists."

Nemesio was relieved that he did not have to ask his friend for a loan; that the offer came freely from Felipe. Details were worked out and hands were shaken. He purchased his eighty, an ugly piece of land, but an eighty never-the-less, needing a team of horses, horse-drawn farm machinery, fences everywhere, livestock, and only God knew what else. Even cats for the barn were needed and the list went on and on and on. So many expenses occurred that updating the house was postponed year after year after year.

Drinking and cooking water was brought over by the bucketful from the Byfields, the first of the few Red Hair friends of the family. Water for washing clothes and for serial bathing was carried up from the Snake River and heated on the kitchen stove. One hasn't lived until one has taken a bath (alone, of course) in the same water in a galvanized tub. (Look at the person next to you; now imagine using the same water for your bath.)

The root cellar, the large garden, and home canning were the family's means of winter survival, along with potatoes from the large spud patches. Beans, both red and white, thrashed the same way the ancient Egyptians did, were added to the family larder.

Oh, how I hated lessons in school about the ancient Egyptians thrashing beans, grains, and the like the way we did. I was sure we would be looked on as old fashioned and backwards as the ancient Egyptians, waiting for a breeze to separate the chaff from the beans. But we survived, some of us anyway. Add to all this, that little event affectionately called the Great Depression (and the locusts, and the jackrabbit plagues) and yet we survived. Add all the payments on the borrowed money just so we could live like the ancient Egyptians and eventually we owned our piece of swampy heaven with a clear title—nobody could tell us to take our serial baths somewhere else.

When we sold our little patch of heaven it still had no inside plumbing, although we had a well dug. The location of the well was determined by an old bearded man with a divining rod. And the government's Rural Electrification Administration brought electricity to rural America and eventually brought us two bare lights which hung from the ceiling of the kitchen/dining room/living room/place. It didn't do much for the family at first, though the new electricity brought us a connection to the outside world through our radio. Probably the most important use was that Dad could now bring in the ewes during lambing so we could provide heat and care for newborn or sick animals. Each of the other rooms in the house received a single bare light bulb hanging in the center of its ceiling. My last serial bath was taken in 1949, the same year I last peed in the stove. (story elsewhere)

Episode 10

Begetting of the Barayasarras

We beget like most creatures do—Nemesio and Victorina did, although not an especially fertile branch of the related gene pool. Married in dual proxy weddings, Victorina came over on a luxury ocean liner, far different from the hog freighter Nemesio did. Sisters, Margarita, Victorina's mother, and Manuella, Nemesio's mother, arranged the marriage between cousins.

No amount of correspondence prepared her for the harsh life awaiting her in the new world; in fact, her life was so difficult that she once wrote her father, asking for the return fare. The next morning, she tore up the letter, deciding to stay, and stay she did, not knowing how much worse things were to become. During those moments, she frequently sang a very pretty, sorrowful song:

Bishop of
Salamanca advised

Rather than
become an errant
student,

It would be better
that I got married

Aye, aye, aye, I got
married I did,

Only to regret it
ever since

For there never
was a shortage of

White thread to
sew black pants

Nemesio also sang a tune but it was more of a teasing of the younger children:

Louie, Louie Leen,
Kaka Pirripeen,

Louie, Louie Leen,
Kaka Tamboline!

Louie was the oldest, the most intelligent, the most generous, and most structured—to a fault. He had to have things in precise order. And yet his own birth certificate had the wrong date. He was born on February 7 but his records show February 6. Mom, who was involved, said that the doctor who delivered him was drunk and listed the wrong date.

Dad opted to name him Bruno, but Mom vetoed that and settled on Luis, which was confused with Lois and/or Louise. He changed his name to Louis John as he had no middle name and did not like the sound of Luis None.

Lou remained a bachelor and lived at a time bachelors did not have many children. He had two acceptable ladies who very much would have married him. "What was wrong with Maria from Italy?" Lou was asked.

"She is too loud and bossy," he told us equally loud and clear, "and besides she has two unemployed brothers living with her! I wasn't about to have three adults around who could talk about me loud enough they could be heard in Italy."

"Well, what about the former nun, Margaret from the Netherlands? She wasn't loud and you can certainly use a prayer now and then."

"I don't have anything—financial, or otherwise—to offer either of them or anyone else for that matter." With that mindset, there were no begets here.

Felipa, as bullied as she was, did have a high school sweetheart—Gordon Berney—red hair, freckles, very curly hair, a pug nose, and a super nice guy. He joined the Navy after graduation and drowned in the Gulf of Mexico during basic training.

Next to come along was 65-year-old Pete, retired from sheepherding and reported to have a bundle of greenbacks. Phil (as Felipa was called) was not interested. "Phil, he's worth mega bucks." That was Dad trying to get her married off.

Felipe Orbe entered Felipa's life and nine months later, Victorina Marie was begat— followed by no more. Her daughter, though, begat three boys, Lucas, Jacob, and Mitchell, whose begetting years are in the future. I do not know if they are practicing in anticipation.

Next in line, I begat two and adopted someone else's "begat," plus raised one with a "made in Morocco" label. Nothing was resulting from our efforts to beget during our first few years of marriage. So we took the adoption route (story elsewhere) only to find that was all it took to awaken our own personal hormones and/or equipment, and we produced, excuse me, begat two. A couple of tubal pregnancies ended at the source.

Christina Marie, adopted, one-half Italian, one-fourth English, one-eighth French, onesixteenth German, and one-sixteenth Dutch, and, in her own words, "One hundred percent Basque." Tina begat a couple—Justina Marie Baire and Vincent Paul Baire, Jr.

Lisa Marie added Christopher Quinn, Zachary Alan, and Alyssa Nichole Whittaker to the begatted.

Mary Ann begatted and produced Christopher James, Nicholas Michael, Michael Joseph, and Sarah Marie Besser.

Brother Frank begat Michael Louis who says he will never get married. Brother Michael was begatless, as were sister Alva and brother Manuel who died as young children.

And that, dear friends, is the reproductive history of the Barayasarra, since coming to America—not the best read in existence.

Episode 11

The Welcome Wagon Comes Calling

"What does this Red Hair want?" Victorina asked aloud to no one in particular, as the man on horseback rode up to the house.

President Roosevelt's CCC program was in full force and the United States was still smarting from the Great Depression. The year 1939 was not the best of years for Nemesio, Victorina, and their four surviving children. The "Eighty" was purchased—just before the big crash—using money saved during better times and from money borrowed from Nemesio's best friend, Felipe Garay.

The Red Hair was on horseback, his once-red, faded, flannel shirt tucked into his Levis and his Levis in turn into well-worn boots. It appeared that the only water ever to touch man or apparel came from his own profuse sweating. His ten-gallon hat was trimmed with a two-inch band consisting of alternating coatings of sweat and dirt. Leather chaps and spurs and a well-worn saddle completed his attire. His horse reacted to his every command like a battered spouse.

"Get in the house, children. Let me see what the Red Hair wants."

"A-low."

"Hello, Mrs. Barayasarra. How are you?"

Victorina said nothing but suspiciously eyed the stranger. "These Red Hairs are always up to something. Probably the one who shot at Nemesio years back. I wish he were here from the fields." She instructed her nine-year-old to ask the Red Hair what he wanted. To herself, she asked, "How does he know our name? I've never seen him before—but then they all look alike. He isn't quite proper."

"Louie, did you ask him what he wants?"

"Mama wants to know what you want."

"Nothing, Mrs. Barayasarra. I know times be hard and you and your man and your young'uns work hard, Mrs. Barayasarra, very hard. I had the missus bake you this sponge cake. I know you can't afford sweets for the children and all, so here, take this."

Victorina, with feet firmly planted, and the initial thoughts about the cowboy still intact, tried to look him square in the eye but still said nothing. Oh, she understood all right—actually she understood English very well, but chose to pretend otherwise.

"Here, take it please. It's all right. The missus made it this mornin'."

"Tell the Red Hair no thanks," she instructed her son, who at nine was spokesman, interpreter, and official mouthpiece for his mother. In his multi-patched overalls, well-worn shoes with holes in the soles and sides, and home haircut he drew himself up with as much authority as he could muster. "She says she doesn't want your cake!"

Then to his mother, in Euskara, "Please, Mama, take it. It looks good. It is free. The Red Hair's wife made it for us."

"No!" she settled it with the boy. "Tell him we appreciate it very much, but no thanks."

"She says she doesn't want it."

By this time, the stranger had handed the boy the cake, turned, and was riding off. "I told him, Mama." Secretly, the lad was not at all unhappy with the outcome. The other siblings were out of the house and all over the cake. Angrily, Victorina swooped up the cake from his hands.

"No! Never accept anything from strangers—especially Red Hairs. Have I not taught you anything?" With that and amid howls of protest, she took the cake, marched to the chicken yard, which was near the house and tossed it over the fence. Her one reason for doing so was the welltaught lesson from her own mother. One never accepts anything from anyone one doesn't know.

This she religiously tried to pass on to her children, and although tempted at the moment, she held on dogmatically. How well she knew her children seldom had cake; how well she knew it was wrong to waste food; and how well she knew they wouldn't understand. Nonetheless, to the chickens went the cake, and into the house she marched the children. "You don't even know anything about him.

Do you want to eat something from someone as dirty as he was?

The wailing tore at the very core of her soul; tore at the very devotion to her family; and tore at the memory of her own mother's lesson. Maybe, just maybe, she was wrong. Maybe, just maybe, this Red Hair was not like the others. Maybe, just maybe... The children's long faces and her own inner turmoil and guilt carried through the rest of her chores. Trying to avoid any reminders of the incident, she put off the gathering of eggs until the task could be delayed no longer. As she opened the gate, she gasped in horror at what was before her. The children answered her call immediately, having never heard such intense urgency in their mother's voice.

"Look! Just look! That is why we don't accept anything from anyone we don't know! Do you understand?" There before them was the grisly demonic panorama of dead chickens upon dead chickens. The cake that killed the chickens had been intended for the family.

The next day, the cowboy rode by, but was never seen again.

The lesson was to survive another generation.

Episode 12

Early Memories—Very Early Ones

Do we all remember the same way? Or do we forget the same way? Why can some remember after one exposure and it takes others repeated stimuli to remember the same thing? Why do we remember some things and not others? Maybe we even remember an insignificant thing such as a small feather which floated down during a third grade lesson about the Panama Canal.

Well, let me search my earliest memories, those which have remained as clear to this day as when they occurred. I am aware of recent studies which suggest that our memories are seldom completely true.

My first example is something I remember as a mental picture. I laid on this comfortable structure that went on forever to each side of me and toward my feet but not past my head—I could not see that way. Several heads (I now think there were three or four) looked down at me from the foot of the bed and around to my left side. These heads, all women, were making pleasant noises which I enjoyed very much.

"Oh, look at that big boy." "Coochi, coochi, coo!" "Baby, baby, baby."

"Oh, big boy, I bet you learn how to harness a horse right away."

All the heads were fuzzy except one at the foot of the bed, my mother. I especially remember her lullabies.

"I can't take you to the dance tonight, the cow has T.B." And the second, "The Bishop of Salamanca told me to go to the convent, but then they decided it would be better for me to get married than to be an errant student. Yes, yes, I got married, I did. And ever since then there never was a shortage of white thread to sew a black dress."

My next early memory involves something I learned through hypnosis. Since my session with the medical doctor who hypnotized patients to get background material, I remembered more details of the event. I was a young man in my twenties when the doctor hypnotized me; the incident I remembered happened when I was two and a half years old.

"James, I want you to hold your hand up. Lower it slowly through what will represent your life from today to your birth. Whenever your hand passes through something significant in your life describe it to me."

I went through fighting with my brother, puberty, masturbation, chicken pox, and other events, somewhat normal. I was down to the time I was two and half years old—and the memories...

"I was weaned off my mother's breast..."

"Why were you two and a half when you were weaned?"

"I don't know, I just was."

European women often nurse their children that long or even longer, as long as there wasn't another child on the way—at least in Mom's day. They may have also believed that one is not as apt to get pregnant while the woman is nursing.

The reason why I was finally weaned was that Mom was expecting Frank. To get me to stop she covered her breasts with garlic.

"The cat shit on my tit." I tried the other and again, "poofie, *kaka*."

"Stink! Oh. *Kaka*," from Carmen, a Basque girl staying with us.

It worked, I was weaned. At the doctor's, he became all excited at the memories that he drew out of me through his hypnosis and asked several questions, trying to ascertain if I had any issues with breasts. Years later, I thought I should have told him that I loved garlic on breasts or better yet, that I love cat's shit on them, but I didn't.

"Mom, why was I weaned when I was two and a half years old? Why was I so old?"

"Frank was on the ... who told you? How did you learn that?"

"Though hypnosis." I was not expecting her response.

"WHAT?" followed by words like devil, hell, dangerous. It was a relief to get back to the weaning discussion. Yes, it was true. She was expecting Frank and had to get ready for him.

Of course, if I remembered being weaned, potty training had to be in my memories. I don't remember the entire process, only one incident when I hadn't yet completed my bathroom boot camp. It may have been shortly after Frank was born, making me an old man of three. This one incident was traumatic for several reasons. After giving birth to twelve-pound plus Frank, Mom became ill with milk fever and needed help while she recovered. Well, help was in the form of Louisa, the prototype for the wicked witches of all fairy tales. Years later, as a teenager, I asked to attend her funeral. I did not do my prayers for the repose of her soul: I merely wanted to see her dead.

Well, she took over, letting Mom know how disgusting it was that I wasn't toilet trained and what a horrible brat I was. She plopped me on a small pee pot, half full of water. If the water weren't there, I would have performed splendidly. However, I did not like the splash and the tsunami potty douche which followed. I refused to oblige and Louisa was not about to let me leave. I won the war of wits even if I sat there for three hours. Finally, she jerked me off the pot, dressed me, and shoved me outside. I immediately went around the corner of the house and did the nasty—in my pants, of course—which I wore the entire day. Not one of my finest hours.

My last of my very early memories included abuse I was subjected to by a lady taking care of us. It is a memory I always had. I had a disagreement with my sister—I don't recall what it was about. She had one doll, a second-hand one at that. Anyway to get even with her, I took the doll to the river and threw it in. The current swiftly took it, as I watched it disappear downstream. Immediately I felt dirty and worthless. I followed, trying to apologize.

Then there she was—the Evil One. I zigged, she zigged. I zagged, she zagged. I zigged, she caught me, and back to the river, accompanied with my screams of resistance and her Satanic, "outsmart me, you little monkey's ass—I don't think so."

She walked me, carried me, dragged me to the end of the plank. She flipped me upside down, grabbed my ankles and dunked my head into the river over and over again. I'm surprised I didn't drown.

"Leave him alone you old witch," from my sister.

"Oh, you want some of the same? Just wait there. Let me bring this one in and then you!"

Felipa turned and ran.

Episode 13

Stand up Straight, Jimmy:
First Grade is Big Time

I looked forward to first grade and school as I looked forward to each and every year of school. Of course, I had the top consulting firm, Big Bro and Sis, there with advice. Opening day and there I was with a pencil box, with two state-of-the-art yellow Ticonderoga pencils with attached erasers (well worth the two for a nickel price over the penny brown eraser-less ones). Crayons, the big box; scissors; ruler, with all the presidents including FDR; even a compass.

"What is this, Louie?" I asked.

"A compass," he replied.

"What do I do with it?" I was full of questions.

"Draw circles," he even knew that. He was so smart. He knew everything.

School clothes were purchased through the Montgomery Ward catalog. The Sears Roebuck Co. catalog, or the Square Deal Department Store. As poor as we were, we were usually better dressed than most. This was at a great sacrifice on Victorina's part.

Grand View Grade School was a two-room school—a big room for grades five through eight and a little room for grades one through four. There were even two restrooms, one for boys and one for girls. One day when the boys were seeing who could pee the farthest, Mrs. Thompson, a girl, yelled in and told us to finish up and get out. Then, even though she was not a boy, she came in and chased the boys out.

It was Show and Tell for first graders. I raised my hand—that is how we let the teacher know we had something to share.

"Go to the front of the room, stand up straight, speak clearly. What do you have to tell us?"

"My mother came over the ocean on a sheep."

"Oh, no, Jimmy. She couldn't do that! The sheep's wool would soak up water and the sheep would sink and your mother would drown." That made me very angry but Mrs. Thompson was the teacher. I decided to take it up with my mother at home.

At recess, I was double pumping on one of the swings with Buddy Towner. He said, "fuck." Since I was trying to learn as many words in English as possible, I repeated it over and over, "Fuck, fuck, fuck."

"Oh no. Don't say it so loud. Mrs. Thompson will get mad and we will be in trouble!" That was enough for me. I'll store it for later.

At the bell we lined up to march in. It was Wednesday and at the end of the day, we had "joke day." Joke day was a time if you had a joke, you told some dumb thing. Then you answered it and everyone laughed—something like, "What is black and white and read all over?" Then you say, "Give up?" If they gave up, you say, "a newspaper." The teacher explains it and she laughs.

I raised my hand and just like Show and Tell, when called on, I went up and told a joke that I heard at recess earlier in the week, "How are seven Jap planes and a pair of woman's underpants the same?" A student gasped, "He said underpants!" The look on Mrs. Thompson's face was not a good sign. But finally she asked, "How?"

"It takes one yank to get them down." No one laughed. And there were no more joke days.

Now, to go out in style—The Hugh Hughes Saga. I sat in the third desk back in the first grade row. In desk number four was Hugh Hughes. I did not look at Hugh since there must be something wrong with him. Maybe it was catching or since we sat close, what if the teacher made an error and punished me by mistake. Every afternoon during quiet study time, Mrs. Thompson went up one row and down the next. Up row two, stomp, stomp, stomp. Then almost a military turn, then stomp, stomp, stomp down my row. Here she comes—STOMP. STOMP. STOMP down MY row. Then, STOMP, next to MY desk. I STUDIED my ass off. She always snorted and STOMP, STOMP, out of the room and then back in with Mr. Thompson and two sets of stomps. STSTOMP. ST-STOMP. ST-STOMP and again, STOP next to my desk. Then again, Mr. Thompson shook Hugh and stomped out—every day the same thing—all year long the same thing.

Episode 14

Let's Scalp Jimmy

Not many memories exist about my birthdays—partly because birthdays were not much different from other days to a family whose chief concern was survival. Gifts, parties, cards, etc. were not part of the day. However, I do remember my fifth birthday when my mother baked a sponge cake. These rare cakes usually were not iced since that merely delayed the eating of it. Lou and Felipa were still at school and Frank and I were at home, although I don't remember any dealings with Frank that day. We probably fought since that was a routine daily event.

Each spring and summer, Johnny Crow, a Shoshone Indian, brought his family from the Duck Valley Indian Reservation, located on the Idaho/Nevada border near Owyhee, Nevada, to the banks of the Snake River. He set up his family tepee on the Totorica lambing sheds grounds just over the property line of our farm.

The Crow family had a boy about my age but I did not play with him. My family did not instill any racial or class prejudices in us—except to distrust Red Hairs and strangers. Indians were strangers, but my reluctance was probably based on the unfair and incorrect stereotypes I had of them from the western movies, which made their way to Grand View via the Wednesday evening movies. I knew that all Indians live in tepees and scalp those who are not Indian. The presence of the tepee always made me nervous.

During an afternoon coffee break, Nemesio was having a piece of my sponge cake with his coffee. He decided it would be nice of me to take a piece of cake to the Crow boy, since about the only people lower on the economic scale than us had to be an Indian family who lived in a tepee and existed on carp, chisel mouths, and other trash fish from the Snake River.

"Take that Indian lad a piece of your cake, boy."

I could not believe my ears. My own father, sending me to get scalped! And Mom wasn't any better—she was wrapping a big piece in wax paper and putting it in a small brown lunch bag. Off I went! Sent to my final reward—by my own parents—and on my birthday! I didn't protest—after all, they did not want me anymore.

Each time I approached the tepee, the squaw, as we called the Indian ladies, came out of the opening, probably wondering, "What is this snot-nosed kid up to?"

And each time she came out, I retreated toward home. When she went inside, I advanced. This forward-retreat ritual went on for several minutes until she finally must have tired and probably decided to remain inside and watch me through an opening somewhere. Anyway, she did not come out long enough for me to take advantage of her absence. I ran to the tepee opening, dropped the bag, and ran like hell for home, falling over the fence in the process.

I managed one look back to see where she was in case I had to dodge arrows or tomahawks. She picked up the sack and said something. I didn't hear what it was but I was not about to ask her to repeat. I ran all the way home and made it without an arrow and with my scalp. "Did you give the little boy the cake?"

"Yes."

"What did he say?"

"Nothing."

Episode 15

How to Celebrate a Birthday

Dad was doing his daily chore of feeding the ewes and their lambs, going from trough to trough with a wagonload of loose hay pulled by Jerry and Babe, our team of horses. If we weren't in school at the time, we would help load the wagon as Dad pitched the hay off the stack and then fill the troughs.

The pens, located between the house and the Snake River, were fenced with windbreakers. These were built with two parallel rows of net fencing, about a foot apart and the space between the two rows was filled with tumbleweeds, other weeds, and/or straw, making an inexpensive way to block the cold air and to allow the sun to warm up the air in the pen.

It was one of those days. Louie, Felipa, Frank, and I were at school with Mike the only child at home. The date was February 13, 1946. What was so special with that day? It was the fourth birthday of the one and only unique fourth son born to Nemesio and Victorina. Several things made him unique. He was the first of my siblings to born in a hospital. I was born in Bengochea's Hotel in Mountain Home. Louis, Felipa, Alva, and Frank were born at home or at Guisasola's in Grand View. Frank weighed in at over twelve pounds, making Mom think, "No more of this *kaka*. Any more after this will be in a hospital." So Mike was.

He also liked to wander around. One time Jose Totorica intercepted Mike on his way to town.

"Where are you going, Miguel?"

"Grand View."

"You better tell Mama. Go home and tell her. If she say fine, I'll take you to town. Tootsie, you take Miguel home. He! He, he!" Tootsie, Jose's old sheep dog, understood and started Mike homeward. When

Mike started to turn around, Tootsie blocked his way and let him go only in the direction Jose told him. Even retired sheep dogs remember their performance when they come out of retirement. Jose watched the boy and dog until they arrived safely home.

This particular day—his fourth birthday—Mike decided to help Dad. He climbed up one side of a trough and fell down the other. And then laughed hysterically. Or up one side of a panel gate between pens and again fell down the other side, and each time he did, he laughed out of control.

"Mike, don't do that! You will hurt yourself!"

But again up one side of a panel and over the top and then down the other. And again, laughter of sheer enjoyment.

"Mike, stop that before you break a bone. What is wrong with you? Stop it right now! Do I have to tell you again?" And again Mike paid not one bit of attention and repeated his behavior. This continued as Mom looked toward the pens and saw the performance, "What is wrong with that child?" And then to Dad, "Nemesio, what is wrong with that child? Can't you see something's not right?"

"I kept telling him that he will hurt himself, and to stop."

"Bring that child to me. Something is wrong. Bring him here! NOW!" She was mad now but she was worried, "Now!"

As soon as Dad got near Mike, he knew by the smell what the problem was, "Have you been in the garage?"

"Yes."

"Did you find something in there?"

"Yes."

"What was it?"

"Pop. Pepsi pop."

"Victorina, the child is drunk."

"Drunk? From what? How? Bring him here." He brought Mike toward her and lifted him over the fence. "Phew-yoo. He sure is drunk! Did you give it to him? Where did he get the alcohol?"

"From the garage. I had a fifth out there so I could get a nip now and then without coming in the house. What he did with the rest of it, I don't know. I have to go finish with the sheep." As he started to leave he saw a muddy bottle at his feet. "What the hell is this?" The case of a slightly drunk child and the disappearance of Old Grand Dad and a muddy whiskey bottle was solved. Those mud pies on that plank were not made from the usual water and dirt but were enhanced with ickapoo joy juice.

"Well it looks like I have to bathe and de-stink a drunk four-year-old son of yours before the others come home from school." She cleaned him up and rocked him to sleep.

"Perfect timing, the loaves of bread and biscuits are ready and here they come, my hungry children. Butter and jam are next to the biscuits. Was it a good day at school?"

"Okay. How about here?"

"Nothing here either—never is anything here. Well, there was one little incident—nothing much."

"What was it?"

"Nothing really. Well … Mike got drunk!"

"DRUNK?"

"Mike got drunk?"

"Way to go, Mike!"

Episode 16

Most Teachers Are Good
This One Missed the Mark

Somewhere else I said that the teachers were not questioned and because of this, we learned to solve our own problems. The following account is the downside of this position. My brother, Mike, was a Sophomore in Meridian High School and although not an A-student, was probably a B/C level, but certainly not an F-student. Mike did not say anything about the grade, the teacher, or pushups until several years after he had graduated from school.

At this time Mike was extremely obese and was teased about it by the other students and also by the teacher. In addition to Mike, another student was extremely obese and he, too, was ridiculed by teacher and class. Both had an F for their Sophomore English semester grade.

"Do you want to do some extra credit to raise your grade to a passing grade? That way you won't have to repeat the entire semester next year," Mr. Carson Gault asked, seeming to make an abrupt change from teaser to helpful friend.

"Yes," said the other student.

"You, Mike?'

"Yes."

"Okay, Big men, to the front of the room. Drop down and give us twenty pushups."

Eddy started and of course the class howled laughing as he struggled. "Come on, Fatso."

"Mike's a chicken, pluck, pluck. Lay an egg, Mike,"

"I said I would do extra credit. I'm not making a fool of myself to make you laugh. I'll repeat the class. I am not surprised you won't be back next year."

"Show some respect, young man."

"Earn it! Do twenty pushups."

Episode 17

25 Cents is 25 Cents

"Jesus Christ, Phil! How could you be so stupid? You swallowed two dimes and a nickel—a whole 25 cents?"

It was sometime in the 1940s and sister Felipa did indeed swallow two dimes and a nickel, an emotional and financial crisis for the children of a poor immigrant family who was still smarting from the effects of the Great Depression.

25 cents were not small change to Felipa and her siblings, who were not being very sympathetic to her plight. No concern was expressed that the coins may cause her any harm—only how she could have been that dumb.

"It's not the end of the world! Almost—but not the end! *Jesus, Maria, eta Jose!* What went in will come out." Mom answers, more in response to the commotion the siblings were having than to the temporary journey the coins were taking. "They will come out!"

"In the outhouse! I'm not going after them there."

"No, I didn't say that! You do your thing out in the yard behind the house. Take an old coffee can filled with river water. Use a stick or a shovel or a hoe—Do I have to figure it all out for you? Wash the coins off and bring me the coins with new clean water. I'll boil them on the stove with a strong chlorine bleach mixture."

"I wonder if John Bulish swallowed those coins before you did and had to do all that. I bet they came from John Bulish's *kaka*," Lou teasing Phil.

"And he doesn't live in a cave with a mother to boil them in Clorox either," I added.

"John Bulish's *kaka* tastes mmmmmm good."

"Quiet. Both of you. And stop crying Felipa. That's enough, you two, or you will be the ones to clean them." The thought was enough to quiet us down—at least when Mom was around.

The coins were eventually returned to Felipa, slightly discolored, but still worth 25 cents with or without John Bulish.

Episode 18

Joe Louis—Champ—Best Friend

Joe Louis, heavy weight champion of the world, the brown bomber, Dad's hero, and the favorite of ours during the 1940s, even though many white boxing fans rooted for various great white hopes to defeat the brown bomber. Dad liked to support winners and it was hard to see the champ as anything but the champ.

When a ewe had triplets or did not have enough milk for three lambs and there was not another ewe which could raise another lamb, the lamb had to be bottle raised. These lambs were called bum lambs. Joe Louis, a black lamb, was to be bottle fed, and therefore a bum lamb—not a bum in any derogatory way. We loved Joe Louis, the Brown Bomber, the boxer, and we loved Joe Louis the lamb so we named him the best.

No one was ever mad at Joe Louis. Well, that's not true—the lamb, Frank, and I were in trouble at least once. Let me relate what happened and see if you agree if Mom was too harsh on us.

Mom's old foot-operated Singer sewing machine was always in use. In addition to the regular patching of clothes, Mom found a way to use almost everything that she had at her disposal. Scot's Best Flour sacks were saved and sewn into aprons, if nothing else. Whenever a choice of print was available, she insisted on the white sacks with red pinstripes spaced about an inch apart. When she had enough of these on hand, she made ruffled, princella type curtains for all six tall, narrow windows in the kitchen/multi-purpose room. She fancied these up to the point that the horizontal seam needed to join two sacks together for the length of the window was not offensive. Although she never said so, she had to be proud of these curtains. They cost nothing over the cost of the flour and time invested, they were better made than store-bought curtains, and they replaced the disintegrating see-through curtains with the multi-colored polka dot tufts. Felipa Uriona admired them so much she decided to save the same print and make similar curtains for the Wood Creek Sheep Company cook shack.

Mom's curtains were nice but they were showing wear so she bought store curtain replacements for the outrageous amount of five dollars. She hesitated using them because of what Dad would say, spending so much money. Finally with enough nerve, she did—and newness really perked the place up.

Now the plot thickens with our folly: we pushed Joe Louis into the house. The champ went window to window and ate the bottom foot of each curtain. He was on the last curtain when we heard mom's litany. We learned she could either speak Basque, Spanish, and English all at the same time or the woman could speak in tongues.

Scot's best curtains went back up. There was no need to upset Dad with the cost of the curtains in the trash so the Christian thing was done and he was spared the upset.

And although Joe Louis received a whack of Mom's wrath and her broom, he soon forgave and forgot since he was a good Catholic. (I know he was Catholic since at church, I heard the priest speak about THE LAMB OF GOD.)

Life continued and at times when the lamb was laying down chewing his cud, Frank and I lay down with him using his wooly belly as a pillow. His lower jaw rotated as he chewed his wad of cud. When the chewing stopped, he swallowed and we heard the chewed cud go down. After a bit of silence, we heard a rumble coming up his esophagus. This was again followed by the circular jaw motion. And again. And again.

"Where does cud come from and where does it go? What was cud?" I asked Frank, even though I knew he didn't know or care.

"What! Wha-at? Who cares?

"Come-on. You hold his jaws as he chews. Let the jaws move. Just be ready."

"What are you going to do?"

"I'm going to look down his throat and see for myself! When we hear the new cud coming up, you open his mouth. I'll tell you when."

"Okay, but you sure are dumb. This I gotta see!"

"When I hear it come up you open his jaws?'

"Dumb. Dumb. Dumb."

"There's the rumble. NOW!"

Frank opened the jaws. I looked, my eyes right up at Joe Louis's mouth. The cud came out.

Yes, it did—in my eyes, up my nose, and in my mouth. All over me. Joe Louis jumped up.

Frank ran off laughing, "Dumbass."

Joe Louis, who was the largest of our lambs, was so tame and halter-trained, which unknown to us gave him a career for years to come. Fred Korner, boss of the Bruneau Sheep Company offered us six ewe lambs in exchange for Joe Louis, since the lamb could be a bellwether leading sheep. With much sadness, we accepted his offer to spare his life.

Unfortunately, that was not to be: A hay truck backed over and killed the champ a couple of weeks later.

We cried, of course but we received another lesson of hard knocks.

Episode 19

Banderas, The Rotten Egg, and I

"Mama where do eggs come from?" I asked of my mother.

"From chickens," she answered.

"But how, Mama? How do chickens make eggs?" I asked again.

"Well child, they do it sort of like going to the bathroom. The eggs come out their *kakaleku*."

"Ugh! I'm not eating any more eggs."

"Why do you think they have a hard shell? That's going to keep them clean—and you don't eat the shell!"

That was reassuring about the shell but then I began to wonder about the rest. "Are you sure about the *kakaleku*, Momma? Why are the eggs in a nest?"

"Child, you have too many questions for a busy old lady! Go to the hen house and ask the chickens, or better yet, go and see how they do it! There goes Banderas. Go sit on that orange crate and ask her." She probably considered this a stroke of genius on her part—it would get me out of her hair and should keep me busy for a while.

I pondered the suggestion for a while and decided it wasn't too bad an idea. This may have been an early warning of my later interest in biology. I went to the hen house, plopped on the crate in front of Banderas, and we stared at each other for what seemed like days. I was very quiet since I assumed that this must be a very private moment for the hen. "I wouldn't want someone carrying on watching me if I were the egg layer!" I thought to myself. At times, I would quietly root her on, "Come on Banderas, do it!"

But she seemed to be in no hurry and sat in her nest of straw, staring back at me, probably thinking, "Why don't you leave, Kid, so I can do my thing?"

I imagined a thought conversation to go on as follows, with the hen thinking in chicken thoughts and me in people ones:

"Come on, Banderas, do it!"

"Go away, Kid, this is private!"

"Come on Chicken, do it!"

"Go away Kid, this is private!"

I was sure the hen thought of me as Kid since there was no way she could know my name.

Finally, some movement. The hen stood up in the nest, still glaring at me. She then squatted her rear end down and made a little grunting noise. The egg slid out into the nest as she settled back on it. She seemed to be relaxing and I imagined that her *kakaleku* was puckering in and out as she recovered. Banderas then got up, flew to the ground from her cubbyhole nest and started the "I've just laid an egg!" cackle, except this one probably said, "I've just laid an egg and my goofy friend watched me the whole damn time. Is he all right?"

Little did Banderas know that her importance in my young life was far from complete. We had no rooster so, of course, any eggs laid were not fertile. Hens still could become "setting" hens. If free to roam, they would find a location and lay a clutch of eggs and then sit on the eggs, using their body heat to hatch them. That's fine if eggs are fertile—in 20 to 21 days the eggs hatch. Banderas sat on her clutch of eggs: 21 days, no babies; 31 days no babies; 41, 51 … no babies. "It ain't gonna happen, Banderas!"

During the forties and into the fifties, there were government agricultural programs designed to help control prices. Some, like the Soil Bank, which paid farmers not to farm part of their land, we chose not to utilize. It turns out that it was mostly the large commercial farms that profited from that program. A second program did affect us. The amount of acres of certain crops was limited. Oats was one and we had sixteen acres over our limit. We could not harvest it as oats, even though Dad could use it and still have to buy more.

One of the choices was to cut it for hay which Dad did. In the process, the mower killed a mama pheasant the day her chicks were hatching (if I were a graduate student of Biology at the time, I could have written a paper on imprinting.) I caught all ten chicks and became the stork carrying Banderas' babies to her. Immediately, she began clucking, trying to call them to eat, but they wanted none of her. I left for the field with Banderas trying her best to be a good mother, but her babies not responding.

Two hours later, I ran to the coop. Success. Banderas was sitting down with her wings spread out, protecting her babies as they peered out from her feathers. Banderas was proud as she strutted past the other hens sitting on their rotten eggs. Even though eggs were scarce, it did happen at times.

Little did she know what was in store for her with this generation, but she was happy and they were healthy. She took them to places never seen by pheasants before; under our porch, in the garden, past our dogs. As nice a sight as that was, it was not quite the survival techniques needed in their world.

In the meantime, as they matured and could fly, they flew across our cow pasture as Banderas ran along below them, scolding them, ordering them to return to the safety of mother ground. "Come down this minute before you fall from that height and break your necks!"

They would land at the far end of the pasture and wait for her to catch up, then SWOOSH! Up again and back to the original end with her objections, the entire way back.

The adoptive mother's care was the reason all ten grew and matured, whereas in the wild, predators and the difficulty of finding food would cut the success rate down. Ultimately though, the very things—humans—that helped her at one point became the fatal flaw at another. Humans had fed and enjoyed the chicks, which then enabled other humans to hurt them. The first day of hunting season saw a reduction of Banderas's family from ten to one minus his leg.

Banderas was undeterred: she again followed the rotten egg route. A neighbor gave me four fertile duck eggs which I replaced for her rotten eggs. Two hatched. Unlike her children of the previous year, they did not reach their flying age. Instead they spotted a pond so off they wiggled their behinds and swam out to the deep water while Banderas, bless her heart, would step out in the water with one foot, then draw it back and that my dear readers is how the hokey pokey started.

Episode 20

Doesn't Everyone Pee in the Stove?

"Look! Look! There he goes again!"

The Urionas and my parents rushed to the bedroom door to see the event of the century—nay, millennium.

"Why didn't you advertise and sell tickets?" I protested when I later found out that the Urionas had watched me in one of my "mother of all private moments." "Can't a person take a leak without the world knowing about it?"

"Most people don't pee in the stove!" Victorina countered.

As mentioned elsewhere, our house had no central plumbing or heating. In fact, we had no electricity until 1941, at which time we had two bare light bulbs hanging in the big kitchen/dining/living room. The outhouse was located in the chicken yard.

"Push the door shut when you leave so the chickens won't make a mess in there!" was an oft repeated, seldom heeded bit of advice concerning the outhouse door.

Inside the house, behind one of the bedroom doors—for emergencies—was the dreaded ice-cold pee pot. Victorina demanded repeatedly that the boys improve their aim.

Off the kitchen was the main bedroom which then also led to the other bedrooms. A pot- bellied stove with mica inserts on the door was located in that bedroom. This and the kitchen cook stove provided the only heat for the house which lasted until the fires died out during the night and had to be rekindled by Nemesio the next morning.

Besides inheriting Nemesio's nightmare practice, I also followed his lead in sleepwalking. However, I'm sure the spectacular event of peeing in the stove, witnessed by God and half the world, including the Urionas, was my particular innovation.

During the night, some years after I finally outgrew the occasional bed-wetting, I nightly got out of bed, walked to the stove, opened the door and peed into the fire all the while sound asleep. The only time Nemesio objected was if this occurred after the fire had died out and the inside of the stove was still wet.

"Aren't you afraid he'll burn himself?"

"And how does one explain his whistle got burned off taking a piss in the stove?"

After a few more such remarks and a good deal of laughter, the foursome returned to the kitchen table to continue the pinochle game:

"Who's dealing? He does have better aim with the stove than the pee pot!"

Episode 21

Victorina's Wardrobe

The children had to have new overalls for the start of the school year. If new were impossible, then very good hand-me-downs from the older children. The one requirement to which there was no exception was cleanliness—the children had to be clean and had to look nice. This in itself caused some reaction from the Red Hairs.

"How can these Black Basco kids look nicer than our kids if they have so little?" It was bad enough that the Black Bascos out-performed their kids grade wise, but now they were rubbing it in their faces by sending their children to school looking better.

What they did not see was at what price this was accomplished. Victorina seldom went anywhere. She spent nothing on herself. She wore well-worn and patched clothes at home—the entire family did. She wore out Nemesio's old high-top dress shoes at home.

For that rare trip out of the house, she wore the same crepe dress with the painted-on polka dots. The dress was a hand-me-over dress from Eugeneia Alzola. At one time, the dress was certainly very nice with a one-inch ribbon down the front with covered buttons. As the buttons were lost over the years, the string of buttons down the front eventually stopped at the waist for a brief time before disappearing altogether from the dress. The dress was let out or taken in as Victorina's weight fluctuated.

The children noticed this sacrifice on their mother's part. Jim would save up his pennies until enough were saved to order four yards of material at twenty cents a yard. Victorina came to accept this gesture but insisted that the material had to be blue or black with no gaudy flowers, etc.

She preferred polka dot.

Jim saved $2.30 and saw nobody was shopping at the Square Deal Store so he began checking out the material. Abner Holst came over and asked him if he wanted to buy something for his mother. Jim said yes, that "Mom likes polka dots." He showed me red polka dot fabric.

"I'll take it." Jim said.

"The whole bolt?" he asked.

"Bolt?"

"All of it."

"Yes." He proudly answered.

"That will be four dollars and ten cents, young man."

"I don't have that much."

"Did I say four dollars? It's on sale, half off to my big customers. Two dollars and a nickel.

And for you, a pack of gum to boot."

"Thank you, Mr. Holst."

"Mom. I have something for you. Why are you crying?"

"You are such good boy."

Years later, in 1989 when she died, she was buried in a blue polka dot dress. I have the one remaining covered button from the original dress.

Episode 22

Hand-Me-Downs—From Your Sister?

Hand-me-downs are a way of life in most large families. Add the reality of poverty and the way of life becomes either a well-perfected art or an act of sheer desperation. As stated elsewhere, extreme sacrifices were made by the family, especially by Victorina, to send the children to school clean and well dressed. On the home front, at the farm, however, clothes were well patched and re-patched and often served long past the "I've got my money's worth" stage.

My home/work shoes could serve no longer. The soles in both shoes were completely worn off, the side seams had ruptures, the tongue was missing on the left shoe, and the homemade shoestrings had more knots than a rosary had beads. It would be a month before the $1.98 purchase price of a new pair was available to buy me a new pair.

What to do? Felipa had a pair of hardly-worn patent leather dress shoes, complete with buckle and strap across the front. These shoes, more likely than not, were given to the family by friends. I was to wear these—only at home and only until the new work boots were purchased.

"But Mama, they're girl shoes."

"Look, what I've got on—they are men's shoes!"

"But you're my mother!"

"And you're my son!"

"No one will see you. Only around home!"

"I'll go barefoot like the Byfields!

"No, you won't! No child of mine will go barefoot, with all the nails, and animal *kaka* around. Try them on!"

"OW! They hurt! They're too small!"

"Be quiet! How can they hurt? They fit perfectly!"

It was settled. I was to wear the damn things and that was that. I put them on and went out to play with Frank.

"Jimmy's got girl's shoes on!"

Another fight: Victorina settled it by threatening Frank that if he didn't drop the matter, she would find a pair of similar shoes for him as well.

That was hardly much comfort. However much I wished the same fate on Frank, I knew there were no other pair available for him to wear. I left, my eight-year-old manhood was challenged. I instinctively headed for the nearest irrigation ditch and mud puddle. I stepped into the water and with each foot scraped mud across the opposite shoe. Back and forth I scraped and was grateful that patent leather did not take very kindly to mud and water.

I proved one thing—Girls' patent leather shoes will only last one week as work shoes. My new shoes were purchased a little earlier than planned and I oiled and polished those shoes very religiously, making sure mud or dirt was wiped off as soon as possible.

Felipa's outgrown shoes had a tendency to mysteriously disappear into thin air as soon as she outgrew them. Thank God, no one thought of looking through the seats of the outhouse.

Episode 23
The Raleigh Man's Here

"Ma, the Raleigh man is here." By the time he organized his wares in a portable carrier, Mom had some money in her apron pocket. These dealers satisfied a big need, at least in rural America, and especially for families like ours. When getting to the store was an extreme hardship if not impossible, these dealers were there with a partial solution.

We called them all "Raleigh man" even though only one of three sold Raleigh products. It seemed that Mom preferred his brand to the other two. One sold McNess products and the third was the Watkins dealer.

The Watkins seller could speak Spanish and thus had a big advantage over the other two. Needless to say, most of our business went to him.

That is until—until he screwed up. He was on his way to his "easy sale." Did I tell you he screwed up? No one saw him drive up and therefore there was no, "Ma, the Raleigh man is here." He knocked, he said, several times on the kitchen door. When no one answered, he stepped in and went to the cupboard to see what spices were low. When Mom finished with bedroom chores, she entered the kitchen to check the beans on the stove. There she found the man going through her condiments. Now, mind you, she could easily have used Spanish to tell him what she thought— AND SHE DID. She told him in Euskara— YES SHE DID. And the English, she claimed, she didn't know—SHE GOT THE IDEA ACROSS THERE TOO, and at times a mixture. I thought the lady was speaking in tongues. The business Raleigh and McNess did at our place went up immediately.

Episode 24

KKK, My Sheepherder Dad, and I

We all have an awareness and opinion of the Ku Klux Klan, or KKK. Hopefully most see it as the notorious hate group it is. We all know they target blacks mainly, but they also go after other minority groups, including foreigners.

My parents dealt with possible problems by not reporting them to the law. The fear was that the sheriff or perpetrator may be a KKK member. Sometimes the report from other herders was that certain people were in the Klan. Of course this expanded the Klan's influence greater than their actual numbers.

As often as I heard of these accounts, I can't imagine working under this type of pressure. Possibly it may seem that not reporting any happenings because of possible Klan involvement was a coward's way of dealing with things. Put yourself in a herder's situation: You don't speak the language. You are vulnerable alone or with one other person. Rumors that the law may be a Klan member left you with no one to trust. Rather than being a coward, I appreciate the immigrant's resolve to come here and put up with any of this for a better life.

Now before I get to my involvement which was a few years ago in Maryland, let me relate a comic relief yet true story which happened about sixty years ago in Boise, Idaho. The KKK ran a coupon ad in the newspaper, to recruit members in Idaho. Just fill it out with name and address, enclose fifteen dollars as dues for a year, and mail it in. Simple as that if you were a white male, you could become a member of the Klan and keep the undesirable factors at bay.

You are ahead of me if you guessed that a young black man filled it out and sent it to the address given with fifteen dollars. Not only did they accept his money, they made him a member. That's not all, since so few responded, he was declared Grand Poop Bag or whatever the head honcho is called. The now black member took a copy of the ad, the response from Klan headquarters, and a certificate of his acceptance to the newspaper. The newspaper ran the story. Including his picture and interview.

The Klan headquarters threatened to sue the man for fraud—How dare he make fun of the reputable, God-fearing Klan? Anyway for a week or so it was a news item. Threats from the Klan continued, all news worthy.

Then in the height of all the Klan threats, the black man disappeared and no one could locate him. The FBI became involved investigating the situation. It looked like foul play. After a week or so the man was found in California. He had his fun and having no ties to Idaho just moved—at least that was the account which I remember.

Back to the KKK and me: I was teaching at a local college in Maryland. An area farmer was letting the Klan hold a rally on his farm. Before the schedule date several people were making comments in the local paper. I held off since I did not want to help publicize their event. Finally someone described his support of the Klan as Christian. That was more than I could take. To hate is bad enough but to claim a Christian justification was more than I could take. So, I cut loose with my letter, as if it made a difference. No way could it be Christian by doing the devil's bidding. Not the most original idea, I know. But then I made fun of their pointy hoods. They have pointy ugly heads and that was the only hats which fit. Did I do any good? It irritated a few KKK folks.

The day the letter came out, I was teaching a night class. Mary, my youngest daughter, was home when they began to call. She phoned me, scared out of her wits. They claimed they were Klan members. "What did they say?" I asked, trying to assess how serious the situation was.

"Your daddy's lower than whale shit."

"If you want your daddy alive, make him stop writing those letters."

"Your daddy's full of shit."

Just this last year she said one call mentioned cross burning,

"Why didn't you tell me at the time?" I asked.

"I thought you would be upset!"

I left and came home and received two more calls. Late that evening, I received a call from a white Baptist minister and related his encounter trying to integrate his church. "You better be prepared to get this call, this call and on down the list." Mary received the other calls—some were scary and nasty. "You are too late. I already have."

The next day a couple of black ministers called inviting us to stay with them until it all blew over. I thanked them but stayed in my place. The only thing that happened was a rock accidently fell through the window.

Episode 25

Nemesio's Two Cars

It was just before the Big War II. The family had grown to four children (Louis, Felipa, Jimmy, and Frank) and had relied on the Byfields or Basilio Yriondo for transportation. Up until the purchase of the first vehicle, Nemesio was farming the eighty with horses and paying to have seed and stock delivered or produce and fatted animals sold and shipped.

"You need to get yourself a pickup," Basilio advised Nemesio, "What you pay for it can be more than made up through what you'd save in transportation costs."

"But I've never driven a car. I don't know how!"

"That's no problem! Give yourself two weeks and you'll be as good as a race car driver. You'll learn in no time. In fact, I'll teach you—up and down your lane."

Finally convinced, the decision shifted to what kind of pickup to purchase. Advice was asked of Basque friends and very freely given in return.

"Get a used one—since you don't know how to drive—that way, if you bang it up, you won't be out as much," was Emitedio's advice.

"Buy new," was Basilio's response, "You never know what you're getting with an old bucket of bolts! You know, they sold it for some reason. If it were any good, wouldn't they keep it?"

Nemesio listened to all the advice and finally decided on new—a 1941 Chevrolet pickup with compound (first gear). Emitedio's remark about banging it up was the clincher but not in the way it was given.

"You know, Emitedio, if I'm to bang it up as you say, I want something left over after all the banging!"

The pickup was purchased from the Chevrolet dealer in Mountain Home, Idaho. Basilio, who lived in Mountain Home, drove it down to Grand View with Nemesio, as his wife, Brigita, followed in their car. The gravel road from Mountain Home to Grand View was the site of Nemesio's first lesson. Starting was a challenge for Nemesio.

"Pull the choke out a little—not too much! You don't want to flood the engine. Step on the starter while you push the gas down with your right foot. Use your left foot for the clutch. Got that?"

"What?"

"Just watch me. Once it starts, push the choke in and take your foot off the starter. See how it revs up when I push on the gas. Well, you want to be careful about that. Do you follow?"

No response.

"Don't worry, it takes practice. Let up the clutch pedal as you push down on the gas. That's a little tricky at first!"

The directions were repeated several times. Nemesio was sure he had just squandered the $325 purchase price. When the remarks and questions began to expose Nemesio's confusion, Basilio stopped the pickup, got out, and went to the passenger side:

"Now, you try!"

"No, I'll drive around the barnyard when we get home."

"What? And run over a cow or one of your kids? No! You're doing it now!"

Usually a remark such as this would be enough to bring out Nemesio's stubbornness full bloom. This time he did not object, probably because it was his car he wanted to try out, and besides, where better than on the desolate desert stretch between Mountain Home and Grand View?

Directions were patiently repeated. The pickup was started. "Now make sure it's in low gear—down here." Nemesio pressed down on the gas pedal—the truck engine roared approval. He let out the clutch—easy, he thought, as Basilio had instructed. The truck lunged forward, gave a couple of jerks and died.

"Here! You do it! I can't learn. I'll never know how!"

"You did fine! All Basques are allowed to do that once." That became the oft repeated remark from Basilio each time Nemesio screwed up.

"You are doing fine! All Basques are allowed to do that once." "Yes, but that's four times at least, I did that!" Nemesio protested.

"Who's counting? You know Basques only count with their shoes off!"

The twenty-mile trip to Grand View set no speed records. "A cow walking backwards with three legs would be there by now," Nemesio observed.

"And probably a dead one at that!" Basilio teased.

But eventually the instructions and lessons began to take root. The pickup jumped less and less as clutch/gas pedal coordination improved. A few times Nemesio forgot to engage the clutch as they stopped. Some pride began to show when everything was finally done as Basilio instructed.

"Basilio's a good teacher!"

"No, actually Nemesio is a good student. Still drives like a Red Hair, but getting better!" After arriving at Grand View, Basilio and Brigita joined the family for the supper Victorina had ready. As they departed the last minute, "Keep practicing!" was said. As soon as the Yriondo automobile disappeared down the lane, Nemesio and Victorina in front and the children in back, all piled into the pickup. Up and down the lane they went with Nemesio sounding like Basilio as he explained each aspect of driving. He finally allowed Lou to try and was amazed that Lou seemed to know how to drive. He did not know that Fay Byfield had given Lou a few pointers in their Model T Ford.

The pickup became a farm vehicle as well as family transportation. Nemesio still rode with Basilio or Emitedio in funeral processions. On several occasions, manure was hauled in the truck during the day, followed by a drive down to the river to be cleaned for a trip into town or to school.

During the war years, no cars were sold and replacements of family autos had to wait until after the hostilities had ended. Orders had to be placed well in advance and customers were notified as their vehicle was in. Nemesio liked the Chevy—as they were the "best." The new pickup finally came in—the purchase price near $500 this time. Nemesio went in with Lou and the 1941 blue trade in. The dealer in Mountain Home said he made an error in the purchasing price—that it was $525.

Nemesio objected, "We shook on it! When I give my word, that's what it is. It should be the same with you. You said $500."

"I'm sorry, Mr. Barayasarra. I can't let it go for $500. In fact, I have several willing to pay $575 for it. Take it or leave it!"

The dealer was instructed where to place the pickup, ending up with, "What kind of man will not honor his word?"

The children were disappointed—much the same they were the time their mother would not let them accept the cake from the cowboy years before.

"Sorry, kids, but this pickup has a lot of good life in her yet! If a man gives you his word and he shakes on it, well …" He didn't finish the sentence.

It wasn't long after that—about two weeks—that the Ford dealer from Mountain Home heard of the Chevy deal through a mechanic friend of Basilio's. The Ford dealer saw that although this was a poor family, it was strictly cash. He came out to see Nemesio to offer a comparable new 1949 Ford pickup for $500. He assured Nemesio he was good to his word but would sign a contact if wanted.

"No, I gave you my word and you gave me yours. If you screw me like the other guy, I won't buy from you either. And I guess you see we Bascos talk to each other."

A couple weeks later, word arrived that the pickup was in. Nemesio, Lou, and Jim drove to Mountain Home. Anticipation was running high among all three.

"If this one does what the other son of a bitch did, we may be coming home 'red hat'!" "Go and Come! Red Hat!" was a Basque expression meaning coming home empty-handed.

Speculation as to the color entered the conversation. There was no choice of color if one were waiting for the next vehicle. Nemesio was hoping for blue or green. The children wanted green as they had blue.

"With our luck, it will be red or black," Nemesio speculated, with red his least favorite and black his second least favorite.

The three drove home proudly in their brand new 1949 black Ford pickup. "Well, black's not so bad, now that you look at it. It could have been red!"

Episode 26
My Barber Kills People

"Get a haircut before you go to the picture show. And tell them you want it short. We can't afford haircuts lasting less than five weeks. Here's the dollar which should take care of the haircut, movie, and 15 cents for goodies." Mom's advice for me as I got ready for the once a week Wednesday night movie.

And off I went to whoever was coming down once a week to cut men's and boys' hair and to see whatever movie was playing. The barber was Dale Pinder, whose immediate employment history read something like this: last five years, Warden's assistant at the Idaho State Penitentiary, whose duty, among other things, was to be the executioner for those on death row.

Three years before that, Dale was a bartender at the Grand View Pastime, next door to the barbershop. He slept in a storage room at the back of the bar. One September night, after the town had gone to bed, the Pastime was broken into. Dale shot at the burglar from the back room. He fired two shots, which plowed grooves into the bar surface and chased the intruder out the front door into the deserted main street.

Mr. Pinder was sure that the burglar would not come back, so he went to back to bed without checking to see if he hit anything or anybody. The dead body was found the next morning in the middle of the street, between the Pastime and the Square Deal store. Mr. Pinder told the law that he didn't know he hit him since the man ran out the front door.

The new bartender took over at the Pastime and it was thought by most that Mr. Pinder was serving time. Instead, he was serving as the official executioner for the state of Idaho.

All I could think about as he cut my hair was, "Gee, This guy kills people—more than one." And he would chatter without let up about my love life, that I should be out there getting my share of ass and not let Paul Spang be the only one acting as town stud. And, of course, that made me more nervous. When he finally splashed that good-smelling stuff on my head, he let me go with one last comment, "There is a lot of good-looking girls out there. If Paul can get it, why not you?"

Whether the wanderlust got him again or if some parent complained about his conversations with their son made little difference: Mr. Pinder was off again with a new career.

The next barber was another in the line of losers to cut hair. I'm sure this gentleman had plenty of *couth,* but he had that phony pious smirk that so many ministers have—you know the ones that have to tell you when they were saved and they were born again—in case you can't see it. He was the local minister, was trying to farm a small farm, and he accepted the Wednesday evening barber gig.

Anyway, after a short and undistinguished career in Grand View as minister, farmer, and barber, the reverend eventually sold his acreage and moved to a different church. Grand View was looking for a new barber again.

"Get a haircut before the picture show. Here's a dollar, which should be enough."

"Mom wants it shor... Oh, hello, Mr. Pinder."

Episode 27
Things to Fill Up the Time
a Busy Lady Doesn't Have

When the occasional sheep, calf, or hog was butchered, the fat was trimmed off and saved until enough was on hand to process. The hog fat was rendered on the stove to produce the lard to be used in cooking anything fried. Other fat, from the various animals, was eventually used in making homemade soap.

The smell from these two activities made me sick and I dreaded these events as much as I dreaded the painting of the kitchen. These were two of the many allergies I was plagued with.

"How will I ever survive as an adult if these smells, and tasks such as thrashing grain, chopping hay, etc., make me so darn sick?" In my world, where everyone I knew lived on a farm, where these events were routine and unavoidable, this was an unvoiced, but legitimate, concern of mine.

The tasks of rendering lard and making soap were Victorina's, which she had to manage in her usual daily routine. The children were to be watched—especially during the added dangers from the molten fat and caustic lye of the soap-making. She prepared three full meals a day—even though the menu varied little from day to day: red or white beans with potatoes and cabbage if available from the garden, fried potatoes with green peppers, again if in season from the garden. In fact, summer times were good as the garden produced much to supplement the beans and potato basic diet.

Clothes were washed by first boiling them in tubs on the stove and then followed by hand scrubbing on the washboard which was hard on knuckles as was the homemade soap used. The washboard was eventually replaced with a wringer washing machine. The clothes were hung on lines strung from tree to tree in the yard. These were gathered when dry and then dampened and rolled up to await the ironing. Victorina ironed everything, using two alternating irons which were heated on the kitchen stove. Everything ironed meant everything—dish towels, bath towels, bedding, handkerchiefs, and even underwear. If Nemesio prided himself on his straight rows in the field, Victorina prided herself on her neatly ironed laundry. She oft repeated, in disbelief and amazement, what one of the Red Hair ladies said about some new sheets the lady had purchased. This remark was especially interesting because it was made in the day when sheets were supposed to be white:

"I bought these new sheets—black ones. They don't get dirty like white ones do. Why, I've had them on the bed for two years and haven't had to wash them yet!"

To which quote, she added, "How would you like to sleep in those sheets?"

Homemade quilts were made from wool which was washed, sundried, and carded. This process was repeated until the wool was completely cleaned and free of any debris. The wool would then be spread evenly between layers of cheesecloth, sewn loosely to keep the wool from separating and matting. This was then covered with a cotton flower print, held in place with little bows of knitting yarn spaced about six inches apart. It was these quilts which kept the sleeping family warm during those nights when the temperature dropped below freezing in the house. When the cover needed cleaning, the bows were cut and the cheesecloth-covered wool removed. After cleaning and ironing, the cover was resewn to the cheesecloth/wool insert, with bows replaced. If the wool needed to be cleaned because of bed-wetting by one of the children or because Victorina felt it was time to clean it, the entire quilt was taken apart and the entire process repeated even though less carding was needed this time.

These special activities, lard-rendering, soap making, quilt making, etc., had to fit into her daily routine duties. Oft times, many of these activities carried well into the night, after the rest of the family went to bed.

For example, the lard-rendering often did. The melted fat was strained through a colander and cheese cloth. She insisted on the cloth to remove even the smallest particle from the lard. The lard was then poured into four-pound Hills Bros. coffee cans to harden.

Soap-making involved the additional risk around the children since caustic lye was used in the process. Older children were recruited to watch the younger ones.

Looking back on all these activities, this busy schedule may have been one of the reasons Victorina so rarely left the house. Grocery shopping was done through the children. Even though she relied on the children to do the shopping, she had her preferred brands: Scots Best flour, Hills Bros. coffee, pure cane sugar, and Mazola oil.

Yes, Victorina was one busy lady. She was thoroughly amused and enjoyed the report Lou made of a conversation overheard in the town barbershop.

"My wife is so tired today—she canned three quarts of tomatoes!" the barber related to his customers.

That very day, Victorina canned 114 quarts and 32 pints of tomatoes. She loved hearing that story which she followed with the black sheet account.

Episode 28

How to Not Fool a Basque Lady

A yard around one's house with more than twenty cottonwood trees provides one with plenty of shade in the good ole' summer time and with plenty of leaves to be raked and removed in the fall.

Regularly, all dead trees were cut down and live trees were topped to keep them under control. The wood from this endeavor was added to the woodpile, a major source of energy for the kitchen cooking stove and heat from the potbellied stove, located in the middle bedroom. Middle bedroom literally was the middle bedroom with access only through it to the other two.

The leaves that surrounded our house seemed to have little value once they had fallen to the ground. We had a drain ditch that had been dug to drain a swampy field that had a huge eroding gully, which if left unchecked may have provided insight as to how the Grand Canyon came about. Apparently, Dad had little interest in academic research and, therefore, took on the goal of slowing down the rate of erosion, by relocating the dead, worthless leaves from the yard to the gully.

This provided a job for a couple of idle members of the household, namely my brother Frank and me.

"Rake the leaves into large piles: Louie or I will haul the leaves to the gully with the pickup tomorrow morning," Dad instructed us, adding, "Don't pile any leaves over the septic area." Why we had a septic tank area was beyond me since the house had no plumbing, but we never asked.

We started raking, making the piles as large as we could with the least amount of effort, as we had the year before and the year before that, and back to when we weren't any good even for that prestigious occupation.

In the yard was also an old cot with sides which could be raised up, making a double bed. A mattress with repeated pee stains, smelling of Clorox bleach, covered the wire net sides. It was impossible to sleep even two children in it, since any time one child got out of bed on his side, the cot would tip over dumping the other on the floor on the other side—one of the few forms of healthy diversion available for pre-television, pre-historical times. Finally, it too was hauled to the erosion modification war games.

"Hey, Frank, let's prop the cot on four legs with the sides extended and pile leaves on top and see how high a pile the leaves will make if we make one huge pile. It will be cool," my alwaysworking mind suggested. I am not sure I said kool with a "k" or with a "c"—I think it was with a "c"—Oh, I bet I said, "It will be fun."

"Are you crazy?"

"Come on, Frank. It will be fun. We can take that old cot, put wood blocks under the feet to elevate it, cover it with leaves, and we'll have a secret hideout under it all."

Finally convinced, the old cot with loose and missing springs was propped up on four logs. Two sides were covered by draping burlap gunny sacks down to the ground. The task of hauling the leaves began. As the pile grew, it became more of a challenge—could we get all the leaves in one pile before Dad came with the pick-up? Periodically, we would pause and dive into the pile and under the cot. The leaves would fall in behind us covering our point of entry.

"You boys be careful." Mom could always be counted on to say something like that. Of course, it was ignored as one of those Mom-things to say.

Finally, the last basket of leaves was thrown on the pile—a pile fifteen feet high and twenty feet in diameter. Diving into the leaves was even more exciting than we imagined since by now we would have to crawl several feet in the soft dark leaves to get to the hollow space in the center. We even got our sheep dog, Tootsie, to follow us in.

Eventually, we became bored with the game and were just about to abandon it for something else.

"Let's go fishing," Frank suggested.

I was about to agree when I thought of one last use for the pile of leaves. We knew Mom had been watching us play in the leaves. We knew Mom could be fooled since she always commented that one or the other of us would never reach adulthood since we fought so often. I was to hide behind a nearby wooden fence as Frank would start cussing me and jabbing the leaf pile with a pitchfork. I was to cry and scream as if I were being stabbed by the fork. When Mom would come running out of the house, I would step around the fence and we would laugh at her, "Ha! Ha! We fooled you!"

"Okay. Got that? Wait until I get in place. Okay. Start poking the pile."

"Take that, you Jerk Head," Frank began. "I'm tired of you bossing me around!"

"Ow! Ooo! Ooooo!"

"Take that, Asshole. You won't be bothering me anymore!"

"Ow! Stop! I'm bleeding! Ow! Ooo!"

Out she came, as expected. "Jesus, Mary, Joseph! What on earth?"

I looked through the fence. She flew out of the house—at three times the speed of light. I saw the look on her face—immediately realizing we had gone too far. No way was I about to complete my part of the charade. I took off, leaving Frank to fend for himself.

"Jim. Jim. Come out!" "Mom, he's on the other side of the fence!" "Jim, come out! It's not funny, Jim!"

She grabbed Frank and began digging through the pile of leaves.

"Jim, come back!" "There he is, Mom!" Frank pointed as I was seen just rounding the corner of the barn.

The willow switch was once again applied. I wondered if the pitchfork, itself could have been any worse.

"Jesus! Mary! Joseph! Jesus! Mary! Joseph!"

Episode 29

Rudolph, the Red-Nosed Reindeer

I hated Rudolph the Red-Nosed Reindeer—I mean, I really, really, REALLY hated Rudolph the Red-Nosed Reindeer—well, you get the idea, I didn't like him.

"If one or the other of you survives to adulthood without killing the other, it will be one of heaven's miracles!"

Among Mom's many chores, one of the most regular was refereeing the almost daily fights between Frank and me. There never was a shortage of reasons to fight. An innocent playtime could immediately become a killing field moment. For example, the splitting of a nickel five-stick pack of gum was reason enough to erupt into a vicious free-for-all over who got the larger half of the stick which had to be split into halves—or even who licked more of the wrappers the gum came in. Unimportant as these seem now, they were definitely matters of life and death then.

The mother of all fights between the two of us occurred a week before we moved from Grand View to Nampa. I was sleeping while Mom was getting ready to do the laundry. She had the clothes sorted and piled in appropriate piles next to the bed: whites, colored shirts, Levis, work socks. Why were the clothes next to my bed, I don't know. All had to be washed in water carried up from the river and heated on the stove. She had a system to make best use of the water to go as far as possible: Whites and fine clothes first, then colored, then darker colored, and finally the work Levis and socks—that is if no bleach was used along the way. Whites had to be rinsed with bluing. And this with a ringer washing machine. It kept Mom off the streets.

Frank was being a turd tickling my face with one of Dad's dirty sweaty work socks. I brushed each sock off as he laid it across my mouth. I eventually woke up as he laid another nasty sock on my face.

"Stop it. Goddamn it!" The next sock hit me in my open shouting mouth. "You asshole!" I took the sock and threw it back at him. He backed off to the doorway. The sock was too light and didn't reach him. Then to make matters worse, he added insult to injury by swinging his hips from side to side, singing, "Rudolph the Red-Nosed Reindeer had a very shiny nose!" Innocent fun and teasing? Not to me. I was very touchy about any reference to my big nose. My mother's nose although big was bent like Dick Tracy's. Dad's stuck out there a mile and a half—like mine. I spent hours on end pushing in on the end of my nose—hoping it would become more like hers and less like Dad's.

The socks I threw it back at him were too light and didn't reach him as he had retreated to the doorway. "Rudolph, the Red-Nosed Reindeer had a very shiny nose!"

Another reference to my nose I did not tolerate was "Pelican Nose, Peak-ed Beak!" coined by Lou which Frank also delighted in using against me. It was a moral victory of sorts to be the first to use that remark against the other.

Anyway, there he was, "Rudolph, the Red-Nosed Reindeer had a very shiny—BIG RED—"

"Shut up!"

"BIG RED Nose."

I threw another sock but it too fell short of the mark. I reached down to the floor and grabbed an old work boot. I threw it and it promised to be a perfect shot. It was heading right for that bastard's head.

Mom, realizing that things were getting ugly, decided, "enough is too much," and stepped around Frank to intercede. She didn't see the shoe coming and what was meant to hit Frank hit her instead. She winced in pain.

Neither Frank nor I came to her aid. Instead our fists and words flew.

"Look what you did, Asshole!"

"What I did? You threw the shoe!"

"You started it! It's your fault!"

"Is not!"

"Is too! Pelican Nose, Peaked Beak!"

"Is not! Pecker head!"

I'm not sure who finally stopped the fight, probably Mom. Anyway, when the new neighbors, the Asumendis and Badiolas met us, Mom had the entire right side of her face black and blue with her eye swollen shut. I don't remember our punishment but I've often wondered if our new neighbors looked at Nemesio as a wife beater.

Did I tell you I hated that song?

Episode 30

Four Friends Fur Finders

The Byfields were "Red Hairs": but they weren't "Red Hairs," if you know what I mean. They were our friends, and were always there to lend a helping hand to us when needed, as we were for them.

For example, they let us get our drinking water from their pump. Water was carried from their pump to our house by the bucketful. Our drinking water in a pail sat on a kitchen counter with a community dipper. Not to be outdone, Dad would send them vegetables from our garden or a front quarter whenever a lamb was butchered.

On our bank of the Snake River, we had a lone willow tree which a beaver was in the process of cutting down. John and Bob Byfield, along with my brother Frank and I, decided to trap the beaver by setting an old coyote trap near the tree and covering it with wood chips. We would wait overnight to catch the beaver, sell the hide for tons of cash, and divide our windfall four ways. Presto—easy street—endless supply of new toys and bubble gum! We, the original four, declared ourselves original founding members of *FOUR FRIENDS FUR FINDERS*.

Since the tree was on our farm, Frank and I were to check early in the morning to see if we caught the beaver. If we did, all four would get together and go from there.

Not waiting for Frank to wake up, I rushed toward the tree through the sheep corral. "Oh, my God. There is something moving down there. Yes! We got him!" I rushed back to get Frank and tell him the good news. "We got it! We caught the beaver!"

Frank was up and off; we went over the fence and down the hill.

"There, there it is." A few more steps and we stopped dead in our tracks. Yes, there was something down there. Not brown like a beaver but white like a ewe.

"Holy Shit! One of Dad's best ewes! We had better get it loose before Dad finds it." As much as we tried, the ewe was in no frame of mind to let us get near her. The river being high, and the ewe butting us, we were afraid we may fall into the river.

There was nothing left but to confess our folly to Mom.

"Mom, you know that willow tree the beaver has been working on?"

"Yes, why?"

"And you know Ed Towner goes up and down the river and hauls a boat full of muskrat and beaver hides back?"

"So!"

"And you know how expensive fur coats are?"

"Go on! I don't have all day!"

"Well, we set a coyote trap by the tree to catch the beaver, to sell the hide to make a lot of money. We caught one of Dad's sheep instead."

"*Jesus, Maria, eta Jose!* You two are going to be the death of me yet. If Ed Towner catches a boatload a day and still is about the only one poorer than we are, what were you going to do with one beaver skin? Louie, go down to that willow tree and free the sheep your brothers have caught in a coyote trap. Quick, before your father finds out. *Jesus, Maria, eta Jose.*"

Louie freed the ewe, its leg broken. He threw the trap into the river, "that was about the dumbest, stupidest, most idiotic thing anyone has ever done. You had better be damn glad; no one is going to tell Dad."

We took the tongue lashing quietly, thankful that Dad would not know. We went home for breakfast.

Dad came in a little later, "Come on boys. Get some shingles and some rags. One of the ewes has a broken leg—we have to set it. I'd give anything to know how it happened."

The "Four Friends Fur Finders" had a corporate meeting and went out of business, after less than 24 hours of existence.

Episode 31

The Manly Art of Crocheting and Fisticuffs

"You don't want to embarrass the family!" That is what I heard from the "alpha member" when I announced my plans to write our family story. What I expected and wanted to hear was, "That's great, we will all help."

One of my episodes—the breeding of a cow—is included even though all three brothers of mine thought it made Dad look bad: I disagreed then and I disagree now. And besides, now, as the sole survivor, the vote is one to zero.

What does all this have to do with anything? Well, not a hell of a lot—except, I'm going to tell you something about myself that, at one time, I would not. My dad was a self-taught person—at least past, way past—high school level. I wanted to learn something on my own, with no help from anyone. So I chose something I would not ask anybody anything about. Let me give you a hint—is it crocheting or . . . You can see why I didn't want him to know. I can hear him now, "You learned to do that but you still can't harness a goddamn horse!"

I thought my kids would keep my secret. Lisa, at least. Oh no. She told her girlfriends and they tried to catch me at it. Kids nowadays! Now, before you try the Rosie-Greer-does-needlepoint argument to make me feel better, let me tell you, Rosie Greer was a great big bruiser of a football player of my day—Rosie Greer can do anything he wants.

Now, I was a fighter in my day as was my brother, Frank. Every day, just about—no gloves, just bare knuckles—and there we were. These were the real make-you-bleed or Mom's "If either of you make it to adulthood, it will be a miracle" fights. So we both did.

I had an interest in chickens and had a little project going there— probably started when I sat on that orange crate watching a hen lay an egg. I tried crossing different breeds to see how different my chicks were, and my chickens were so different that my dad said it was too bad I didn't spend my efforts raising normal chickens. But you know what? When Mom fried my goofy looking birds, he ate them.

And I raised a garden. Of course it was next to Dad's and the only things I produced were radishes that no one ate. I did have a volunteer tomato plant that I adopted. It produced one giant tomato worm and two small tomatoes, which a toad ate. Damn it all! Why didn't I watch a little closer when the horse was being harnessed?

And I raised rabbits, I did. Like chickens, I crossed different males with different females to get very different offspring. In fact, I had several near orange rabbits that I tried to keep going but then they eventually died off and no more were born. My rabbits and chickens did have a positive effect on the family. Since we had no refrigerator, and meat was hard to keep in the hot Idaho summers. My rabbits and chickens served a purpose: Mom would just say, "I need three rabbits for dinner." I would butcher them.

So why am I telling you now that I can crochet? Because I taught myself and liked what I made—besides, my secret was out. And I don't give a shit who knows, though I still won't do it if anyone is around.

When I got my stitches to be somewhat smooth, I copied simple pictures on graph paper with each square equaling one stitch. Designs were drawn and then made into afghans. Some examples I made were Basque dancers, Greek tragedy/comedy masks, sheep, Uhuru, and others— all given to friends. Others have asked me to make them something for pay, which I will not do. One time I kept track of the hours it took and at minimum wage it came to over $700: I'm not going to charge anyone that much for something their dog will have pups or pee on.

And that, dear people, is why I didn't learn how to harness a goddamn horse. If no one would pay me $700 for an afghan, what do you suppose I could charge to harness horses in my neighborhood?

"But Dad, harnessing horses won't get me very far either—about the same as crocheting, maybe less embarrassing. Perhaps I'll teach."

Episode 32

Father and Son: Terms of Endearment

At school we discussed, *our first job?* Does it mean taking the garbage out to the curb for two bits a pop? Does it mean something contractual like taking the dog out twice a day for $5.00 a week? Maybe it means working at McDonalds, saving for that first car. And I sure as hell hope it doesn't mean running dope on the street corner.

The meaning gets all fuzzy—at least the way I see it. Maybe it is a job and not a chore or duty if it has some sort of training, education or instruction involved before a person can do it. And, of course, if that person can get fired for doing it poorly, then it begins to look like a job.

Yes, I did my part in those non-job jobs. I did take out the garbage but there was no quarter. And I did fork shit from under the chicken roost and calf pens, but there was no pay as such. I did lead a horse up and down the rows in a spud patch with Dad operating a single row cultivator. I did chop the heads off chickens and pluck the feathers off them using scalding hot water.

I did these things because that was expected of me as my contribution to the family I belonged to. Occasionally, I was given a baby calf or bum lamb to raise with all money received from the sale later on being mine to keep. And Mom's fried chicken was reward enough.

I didn't consider these jobs because there was no way to get fired—no matter how poorly I did them. Yelled at? Yes. Fired? No. Yelled at! Oh, you betcha boots, yelled at.

One time, Dad bought several "Springer Black Angus" first calf heifers. One of them gave birth to her calf near a wild rose bush on a hillside pasture. The calf then rolled under the bush.

"Go up and get that new calf out from under the rosebush." Simple enough directions for a simple task. He was busy feeding the animals at that time.

I went up to do my task with all intentions of succeeding. However, the cow had other thoughts, being very protective of her calf. She charged me so I dropped the idea and returned to tell my dad. He was not the least bit happy.

"These goddamn kids aren't worth a goddamn nowadays." And my feelings were bruised by this tongue lashing. He marched up the hill, with his repetitive litany following him like a jet plane vapor trail. He reached to get the calf but old Boss wasn't about to let a big human male do what she kept the little human male from doing.

Again, the cow snorted like she did with me and charged, again like she did with me. Dad jumped, let out a yell and ran halfway across the pasture like a leaning tree hillbilly. The cow returned after about 20 feet, again like she did with me.

And, of course, to me this was poetic justice. So what did I do—I laughed. Big mistake. VERY BIG MISTAKE. Again a repeat of a very familiar litany of expletives colored with added terms of endearment reverberated across the hillside as he approached me towards the bottom of the hill.

But Dad was one to come up with a solution. Since the rose bush was very close to the fence, he found a long pole—well, a long skinny dead tree—and a 4 foot long 2x4. From the safe side of the fence, he used the pole to push the calf out from under the bush, while I hit the cow over the head with the 2x4 every time she charged us.

The calf rolled to safety, the cow returned to her baby, I was relieved, and my Old Man had once again outsmarted nature.

If only I had learned to harness a horse, this would have qualified as a job. What has that to do with anything?

Just everything. It would have been the formal training to make this qualify as a job. Proverb according to Dad was, "If a person doesn't learn how to harness a horse before they become an adult, they never will be worth a goddamn."

Episode 33
The Religionization of Jimmy

A relatively minor incident from my childhood ended up becoming a major turning point in my life. I was about eight years old—the time one would expect a child to receive First Confession and First Communion. To attend Mass meant traveling to Our Lady of Good Counsel Catholic Church in Mountain Home or to the mission church in Oriana, both about twenty miles away. Day to day survival was the order of the day and it was easy to "postpone" this duty.

Basillio and Brigita, Basque friends of ours, gave my brother Frank and me each a monkey bank. It was metal, brightly painted, and would, by no standards, be considered a safe toy today. The monkey tipped its hat when a coin was dropped into the slot. It was a mystery to Frank and me why, no matter how many coins were deposited, the banks always rattled as if there were only one or two coins in them.

It was by accident that we came upon Lou and Felipa using a table knife to fish the coins out. Lou kept us out of the bedroom by holding his foot against the door and through the key hole we could see Felipa fishing the coins out.

"Stop stealing our money, you assholes," Frank yelled.

"Open the door, goddamn it!" I added.

"I'm telling Mom!" What a threat that must have been. "Goddamn you! You …"

I was struck in mid-sentence with a strange feeling. There was something wrong with saying what I did. Even though the anger remained in me and I don't think murder had been completely ruled out, there just was something wrong with using that word. I did not use those words again until my twenties and even then not as a curse or prayer that God actually condemn anyone. I fully believe that one incident was the first revelation to me of God's existence.

By the time I was a high school junior, I became interested in the Catholic faith and sought out lessons. I was treated as an adult convert and met with Father John Paulin, S.M., a Marist priest. I received my First Communion on Easter Sunday of my junior year in high school. I was confirmed by senior year and expressed a desire to become a priest. Lou and Mom wanted me to wait a year. Nemesio was not consulted.

"Why not wait a year and enter next year?" Lou advised and Mom concurred. "Three weeks is a bit blunt for the old man to take. Come with me to Seattle. I have a job at Boeing and you can get one this summer and enroll at Seattle University this Fall."

Reluctantly I agreed. Perhaps I should have accepted the College of Idaho scholarship and attended the prestigious Presbyterian College of Idaho and lived at home. Unlike Lou not receiving the Grand View scholarship with a 4.00 average, I at Meridian High School with a standing of third in a class of 115, received the most scholarship aid of anyone of my class. I turned it down since the shunning was still in play, and I was sure I would be attending the seminary of the Society of Mary in Penndel, Pennsylvania between Philly and Trenton, New Jersey.

During the summer of 1954, I decided not to return to Seattle University but instead, made arrangements to attend the seminary. I still had not told my father. I was afraid to.

"You must tell your father," Mom insisted.

I did and the reaction did not surprise me: "If you do, I'll never speak to you again!" And he didn't for the three weeks before I left. I had to leave at 4:00 a.m. to catch the train in Nampa, Idaho.

"You can't just leave," she said, "Go in there and tell him goodbye."

"He hasn't spoken to me in three weeks!"

"No matter! He is your father!"

Again, I obeyed my mother. I went into his bedroom and touched his shoulder to waken him. "I'm leaving, Dad. Goodbye!"

"Hmph!"

I left his bedroom. "See, Mamma, I told you!"

"No matter! He is your father," she repeated. I hugged her. We cried and I left.

What? You don't understand? My father was Catholic, was he not? Yes, he sure was—wouldn't be anything else. Oh, I'm sorry: I just assumed what was natural to me would be natural to you as well. Let me try to unravel the various levels of cultural differences between us.

With many European men, especially Spanish men, they were Catholic through and through, but many were anti-church and anti-priest. With that attitude in play, let's look at some other issues.

Agricultural jobs aren't the most church-friendly in the economy. Cows don't care if Father Jack's sermon is taking place at the same moment as milking or if the herder is forty miles away at the time. Yes, of course, there are solutions to some of the problems.

However, this next item would be enough to test one's resolve upon hearing your son was going to become one of them. The worldwide flu pandemic was hard on people everywhere. One can imagine the toll it was taking on the young herder populations. A tour of western cemetery tombstones will confirm this with the unusually high number of deaths during the flu season of Basque men in their teens and twenties. Nemesio was very sick—sick enough that a priest was called to hear his Confession and to administer Extreme Unction. Because of the language differences, the confession was not going very smoothly.

"I ees not go for Confessions for all d' time I ees in dees countriees for I worken hills wid a' sheeps."

"When did you come to do that?" Father asked, thinking he was helping the lad out.

"I come tonights."

"No, no when did you come to the United States to herd sheep?"

"I come from de Espania."

"No, no …"

"Yes. Yes. That ees no sins so I no tells dat …"

"Young man, let me help you," the servant of Holy Mother Church continued. "I suppose you missed Mass several times, did you?"

"Yes. I dood dat. And I no help my Ama and Aita in Espania like I needs send mores. I berry sorro.

"How many times did you use a sheep?"

"Alla tine, dat was my jobs—I watch d'sheep. Dat bees my job. Padre, dat ees no sins."

"Young man, yes it is. Oh, I see, my question; you misunderstood what I asked you. Did you and how many times did you fuck a sheep?"

"What you say?"

"How many times did you have sex with a sheep?"

"WHAT—I never fuck d'sheep—How many time you doos dat? I not go confess no more you—You need go more n'me." The door slammed as he yelled, "*Maricón!*"

That explains a lot why no effort was made to have Mike, Frank, and me receive First Holy Communion or to be confirmed. I was baptized Catholic. However, with my godfather later becoming a member of the Congregational Church and my godmother moving to Las Vegas as a hooker, I received little religious direction from them.

Mom praying the rosary was a daily religious activity we saw. She also told us each day which Saint's day it was. My birthday, May 1, was St. James and St. Philip's feast day. Since May 1st is a world day for workers, and St. Joseph was the patron of workers, St. Joseph's Feast Day was moved to May 1st and feast days of James and Philip to another day—and they didn't even ask me about it.

The movie *Song of Bernadette* touched every bit of lint in me. Around fourteen or fifteen, I used to go to a spot along one of the drain ditches on our farm, which I thought was just beautiful, and pray the Blessed Lady would come visit me. I kept one eye on the new grotto in case she did and the other on the pasture in case Dad came instead.

It was time to make the move. I decided to see Father Paulin, but something inside me said I needed to know more about the church first. I asked my sister Felipa. "What do I do when I go to church?"

"Do what everyone else does," she answered.

"Mom, Felipa said in church to do what everyone else does. Is that right?"

"*Bai.* Stand up if they stand up. Kneel if they kneel. Just do what the others are doing."

I did. Okay! How did that go? On the way in, people genuflected: I too—never mind why, I did not know. During Mass I upped when they upped; I downed when they downed; I knelt when they knelt; And I bounced my right knee on the floor as they did—twice, one coming in and one going out. Oh, oh, something was different in the knee bounce ritual as I left. I was facing the lady doing her knee bounce. I am sure it looked cute and that was what she whispered to her husband just before he turned around to look at me. I looked back at Felipa and she was giggling. "I'm not coming back," I whispered to her as we exited.

And I didn't since I was at the age when everybody will remember my mortal sin of genuflecting toward the BACK of the church. Eventually I returned and made an appointment to see Father Paulin. The special sessions for Mike, Frank, and me were great. We were First Communionized and confirmed on Easter Sunday. Now I approached my Father with the seminary news.

A year and three weeks later I left to meet my train to St Louis where we flew to Philadelphia (because that's what the others, Jim Rodenspiel, Duane Sutton, and Tom Akovenko wanted to do). I was on my way to become a missionary priest in the South Pacific Islands. The son of the man who a priest asked if he had ever fucked a sheep was on his way to sanctity.

THE SEMINARY YEARS

I was at St. Mary's Manor, a brand new seminary of THE SOCIETY OF MARY. And just as THE SOCIETY OF JESUS was called the Jesuits, The Society of Mary was called the Marists. Calling the seminary brand new merely meant that the Marists had a seminary in Penndel, Pennsylvania, which they did not have before. They were remodeling an existing building. Well, yes the Marists were remodeling using the seminarians as labor. I am sure the walls I plastered were as beautiful as the Blessed Mother.

As Marists we take three vows: (1) Chastity; (2) Obedience; and (3) Poverty. Poverty and Obedience were the virtues to be learned through the work details described above, but the "best" activity yet to instill poverty—no edible, usable food was ever thrown away. Any grease or fat was used again and eventually was blended in some dish, be it a teaspoon or a gallon. Coffee grounds were used over and over again by adding chicory to the grounds. Needless to say, the coffee tasted like shit. (You don't suppose—nah they didn't, did they?)

If not in class or ceremonies requiring communication, we had a vow of silence in the buildings. No talking at all to anyone except the Fathers. A nod to acknowledge the fellow seminarian was permitted. Anytime I broke the vow of silence, Father Edwards materialized and although he seldom chastised the talkee, he always scared the holy—it was a seminary—out of me.

Since I mentioned Fr. Edwards, let me describe a few of the staff. Fr. Edwards was very intimidating. We respected our inner silent warning system about crossing Fr. Edwards. I think Fr. Edwards was a bully as a teenager and somehow God recruited him. Now he uses these virtues for the Lord.

Fr. Reilly and his big gut. He had what some call a fallen stomach. This kept him from kneeling, genuflecting, sitting, and any bending. And I bet good money, his girl chasing days were in like manner significantly reduced. His choice of after-shave cologne was ineffective.

Fr. Cornelius took it upon himself to decorate the chapel for special functions. He used lots of pink, yellow, lavender, and lime greens, with paper cutouts of flowers measuring in feet rather than inches. I expected St. Alice of Wonderland to visit. What I never experienced was a Fr. Edwards/Fr. Cornelius hybrid decorated chapel.

And now, my favorite is my seminary music teacher. Let me tell you about Father Murphy: Oh let me. How can something so bad be there to make me a better person and a better priest?

There is some singing involved with offering Mass. Let me correct that, there is a lot of singing involved with offering High Mass. But I was prepared to deal with that. What's my problem? Am I vain? No, I am not. My problem is much worse. I have a phobia about it. (MY diagnosis). But there I was enrolled in a college Chorus 101 for credit. And it happened—on day one. The proverbial shit and the cliché-like fan came in extremely intimate proximity to each other.

"James, front and center, up here next to me as I accompany you. Relax, we priests don't bite seminarians who can't sing. Relax, son that was a joke. Learn to laugh." He was doing his best to loosen me up. "Where do you come from?"

"Idaho." I answered.

"Oh, I get those two states mixed up all the time. Idaho and Iowa. Let's have you sing, 'Christ Have Mercy'. Over here, please so I can hear you."

"Kyri ..." came out in my very worst ...

"We'll give you a rest," he interrupted with no explanation. Of course, none was needed. I knew that to start with but nevertheless, I slinked back to my seat, meeting no one's eyes in the process. After the last student left, Father said, "You are tone-deaf and pitch-blind and I have never heard a worse solo. God love you."

"Thank ..." He was gone before I could finish. What do I do now? As far as I knew, I couldn't drop the class—they had no place to put me. So I continued going to class.

Each class would start with a prayer from me. "Oh God, please don't have him call on me," and end with the thought, "I wonder why I wasn't called." Same thing the next time the class met. "Please don't call." "Why didn't I get called?"

All semester long, every class period: "Don't." "Why?" "Don't" "Why?" Why was I now being shunned here?

The semester finally—finally—came to an end, followed by grade reports. I had no hope for a decent grade in Music class. He never called me again after that first and last time. But I opened it with uneasiness. WHAT?

Algebra 101 A; History 101 A; English 102; but where was Music? It wasn't on there, my hard earned "F." Father dropped me from the course but I was not told. I'm sure it was an act of kindness but it was not kind to me. My self-worth was not open for pity. I felt betrayed. I should have been told at the time I was dropped from the class.

A vow of silence existed for all times except during certain activities such as class sessions, official meetings, recreation periods, or to speak to any of the priests. The purpose was to build character and to prepare us for our future vow of obedience.

More than not, it became a way to pull a prank on someone and in this way we followed the letter of the law if not the intent. Before our 10:00 p.m. lights out curfew we would take care of activities such as shaving, bathing, and the like before going to bed. Imagine everyone trying to get all this done using the few sinks, mirrors, and stalls available.

I was always impressed by how much noise silence produces, and in getting ready for bed how much of it sounds like brushes—toothbrushes or even razors on stiff bristles. One time as I looked down the line of seven seminarians shaving, I could not help myself. I had a gob of soap in a washcloth and I flung it down the line. The air currents cooperated beautifully. The washcloth flew across the sinks like a magic carpet and just at contact, it tipped and landed perfectly, splat on prepriest face. This launched counter fire with no neutral forces, although some had enough sense to cease and step out into the sleeping area before the super power materialized at the door—the rest dealt with Father Edwards at the doorway with his unholy glare.

Sometimes the envelope was pushed after everyone was in bed along the periphery of the room. One student came from a four-year military boarding school. He was so generic, one might wonder if he were a robot. He was all conditioned and was always the first to adapt. His bed was next to mine and he was always first to finish his pre-beds. He made use of the time before lights out by brushing his shoes. Every night brush, brush, brush. Brush, brush. Brush, brush, brush. Brush, brush. Brush, brush, brush. Brush, brush, every night. One, two, three. One, two. Brush, brush, brush. Brush. Brush.

One night I was ready for him. My shoe and my brush were on the floor opposite of his side. I watched the clock—9:58, 9:59, 10:00. I waited until all sounds stopped. "My gosh," I thought, some people take forever to settle down. Finally all sounds stopped—the last popcorn kernel had popped. I reached down for my shoe and my brush. "Brush, brush, brush. Brush, brush. Brush, brush, brush. Brush, brush, brush." The room broke out in continuous laughter.

All this time, my father's grunt was still on my mind. Finally, my spiritual confessor called me into his office and advised me to leave.

"Go home! If you want to return in two years, we will take you back. Your depression here is not healthy."

I left, wondering what would happen at home. No mention was made of the not-speaking remark, or my stay in the seminary. Life continued as if that year in the seminary never happened.

I decided to attend college during my two-year period. I transferred from Seattle University to the College of Idaho, a Presbyterian college. My only reason for transferring was that the C of I was cheaper and closer to home. All during my undergrad years, I was planning to return to the seminary.

However, a funny thing happened on the way to the seminary: I met Marian Janet Anchustegui, we fell in love, and I married her.

And, there went the priesthood!

Episode 34

Cruising Down the Mighty Snake River

My brother Frank, two years younger than me, was the sibling I most fought—and that out of a brood of seven. I was either two years older than he or he was two years younger than me—I can't remember. Oh excuse me, I said he was two years younger, so that must be what we were. I was eleven and he was nine.

One day we were skipping flat stones on the river surface which bordered one corner of our farm. The weather was warm but the river was high and cold which meant it was sometime in the spring. The river was very dangerous for kids of nine and older youth of eleven and adults as well.

The high water period was a good time to retrieve some of the riches of the river carried from upstream. Our rabbit hutches were built with boards from the river. At times, other items washed ashore, perhaps a piece of metal roofing requiring creativity. Does anyone know how Frank Lloyd Wright got started? I'll bet he lived by a river and raised rabbits.

As we skipped stones, an old dilapidated rowboat drifted ashore. We pulled it in to examine. "Not much water in it; we can bail it out with that Hills Brothers coffee can," I evaluated the situation, "Let's go. We can pick up John and Bob on the way. Let's go."

We jumped in and pushed it out around and away from the fence, which jutted out to close off part of the river for the pigpen. Finally, the river's swift current kissed the boat as her own again. The boat and journey were on their way. And so were Frank, crew member, and me, Admiral Jimmy.

"Holy Shit, Jimmy, there are no oars! And you left the coffee can back there, too."

"You must address me as sir. And you must ask to speak to me, you dumb shit, all proper like from me—and then, not proper like at all, WHERE ARE THE OARS? IT'S COMING IN ALL OVER! USE THAT COFFEE CAN! WHERE IS IT? AND WHERE ARE THE OARS?"

"Sit down. You are going to tip us over. We are going to go over a waterfall and then we will be dead! HELP! HELP!"

We sailed—well, semi-floated—past the Byfields. There never were any oars. Had there been any, we were too young to know how to use them. Had we known how to use them, it would have made little difference working against the river current!

"HELP! HELP! SAVE US!" And if there are no falls in the river, we will end up in the middle of the Pacific Ocean with no paddles and sharks and octopuses, and . . . and things. HELLLLP!"

As we floated down the river. The boat made circles so that sometimes the boat faced forward and sometimes backward. Ahead, the river turned to the right, and cattails that usually grew in a foot of water were now submerged in three or four feet. As the boat began brushing the cattails, however, it slowed down.

"Grab the cattails and pull," I yelled. At first, the cattails pulled apart, but as the boat slowed down, we were able to pull it toward shore.

"Jump!" Frank yelled and was out of the boat. I followed and although the water was over our heads, we made it ashore. Lucky for us, it was not quicksand. We lay on the mud, exhausted.

I looked at Frank. "Leeches," I screamed, "Take your clothes off." There we were, two naked primates de-leeching each other.

"Let's get out of here." And again we took off. And again we stopped to remove more of the nasty things. Luck was with us. We bathed in one of Byfield's irrigation ditches and finally got rid of the leeches and some of the mud from our clothes, then raced for home.

"*JESUS, MARIA, ETA JOSE,*" Mom's reaction, "Whatever happened to you two?"

"We fell in a mud puddle." Frank's stupid answer, but he said so, so I had to agree.

"What kind of fool do you think I am? I wasn't born yesterday morning. *Jesus, Maria, eta Jose.* Well, get some water off the stove and a washcloth off the line and clean that mud puddle off."

As we finished. Frank turned to me and said, "What do we do now?"

"I dunno," I answered, "There is nothing to do. Today was so boring!"

Episode 35

Hog Killing Down by the Riverside

"The pigs are ready. I have two nice ones left, that one and that one over there," Nemesio tells Faustino.

"I'll take that one over there, the larger one. When is the big day?"

"December 14th—two Saturdays from now—not this Saturday, but the Saturday after this coming one. I haven't heard if Emetedio wants one of mine. He always waits until the last minute."

"He has one of his own this year. The reason he brought his own last year was that he was too late to buy one of yours. This year someone left an orphan piglet with him, which he raised. He should have told you. That is what he is bringing this year."

The two men shook hands on the deal and this, to their Basque culture, was as good as a signed contract. The deal was cut. If word got out that a man went back on his handshake, nobody did business with him. And word always got out.

The men were good friends, although there was a time when relations were strained between them. Nemesio remembered an incident from years earlier, so vivid in his mind that it seemed to have just happened yesterday. Faustino ran a boarding house. During the slack period, which followed the shipping of the fatted lambs, the herders often stayed at boarding houses in Boise or Mountain Home, Idaho. Nemesio, while staying at Faustino's, had a bit too much to drink and ordered a cup of coffee. "How much do I owe for the coffee?" A feud ensued. (See "Sheepherder's Day on the Town: Part 2"). Both men eventually got over their anger toward the other. That was then. And now, they sealed this deal the same way they sealed similar deals over the past dozen years—with a mutual handshake.

Nemesio pulled out his Bull Durham tobacco sack, opened it with his teeth, and poured some tobacco into the paper curved by his index finger of his left hand. He then closed the sack with his teeth again, returning the tobacco to the pocket of his well-worn, faded blue chambray work shirt. His shirttails were always tucked into his Levis, with a worn area on his right thigh where matches were struck to light his cigarettes.

Faustino, attempting to distance himself from the sheepherder look, wore dress oxfords instead of high-top work shoes and gabardine pants rather than Levis, a dress shirt rather than a work shirt, and a wide brimmed Panama straw hat to top it off. The distancing effort worked only in Faustino's mind. Faustino pulled out a package of Lucky Strikes, lit one, and made the empty offer, "Here take one of these. I didn't know I had them."

"No thanks, I have one made up."

"Hello, friends. I'll accept your cigarette." Agapito joins the men. And then, to Nemesio, "How may pigs you have left?"

"One."

"None, now." As he extends his hand for the acceptance shake. Counting the one Emetedio's bringing, all eight pigs were now sold and not one asked about price—because that was based on the going rate—the official dressed rate the packers charged.

He passed the jug of *Vino Fino* to Faustino, who lifted the jug to his lips and took a big swig and passed the jug to Nemesio who did the same, and on to Agapito.

As they looked at the hogs, Nemesio took a drag on his cigarette and allowed the smoke to come out of his nostrils. "No more of the pigs like last year's—Hampshires or whatever they were called."

"Yes, I prefer the Spotted Poland China ones," Faustino added— even though neither knew their hog breeds well enough to be sure they were even close.

"I agree. They grow the best—a little lardier than some," as Faustino passed the jug to Agapito. "No, especially as lardy as some of us are," followed by laughter and a coughing spell as he tried to remain in control of himself, "You lika me, I lika you. You no lika me, I no lika you."

Nemesio's sons Frank, age 10, and Jimmy, 12, gave each other a— *did-you-hear-that* look. They liked Agapito, he was as fat as a hog with a face like butchered hog jowls. After a few drinks he could be counted on to say, "You lika me, I lika you. You no lika me, I no lika you." Once the words were out of his mouth, Frank and Jimmy ran behind the barn, not to be seen or heard. Frank would say, "You lika me I lika . . ." and couldn't finish. We were happy we could count on a repeat next month.

Once the last pig was sold, planning started for the event of the year, the annual hog killing ritual at Nemesio's spread on the banks of the Snake River, running through Grand View, Idaho. A total of seven pigs, one butchered for himself, five sold to other Basques, and one to a Red Hair, Fay Byfield.

"Louie, take the pickup and you three gather willow logs and branches. Jose said we could go along the river through his place to do so but to close any gates you open," Nemesio instructed his oldest son.

"How about Byfield's willows? Look how many he has just over the fence," Louie asked his dad.

"Don't gather from Byfield's—Fay said he would bring over a load later," the order was clarified.

"So much for that," said under Louie's breath and then to the brothers, "Come on Bombos, we got work to do. I'll do the driving and you two will open and shut the gates and haul the wood and load the pickup."

"No way!"

"Yes way."

The two younger brothers sat down and refused to move. "All right, I was just kidding. I will help load the wood."

"And help bring it to the truck?" they demand.

"And help bring it to the truck." The acquiescence.

Once the labor union demands and strike were settled, the three brothers quickly had enough wood for the event. They weren't through for the day, however. Oh, no! Nemesio showed up with a lumberjack saw with a handle on each end. Two men, one on each end, pulled the saw toward them when the time to saw was theirs. "Just pull when it's your turn, don't push. Push and the saw buckles—won't work," Nemesio instructed.

The three young men crew adapted surprisingly well. If Jimmy were Louie's sawing partner, Frank stacked the cut wood. If Frank were the one sawing, Jimmy stacked the wood. The wood was cut and stacked—and they were through!

"Oh, no!" from the three boys, almost in perfect harmony, as if rehearsed. Fay, his wagon, and his team of horses came with a load, reaching halfway to the moon.

"Good timing, Fay," Nemesio said to Fay and then to his sons, "You have enough daylight left to get Fay's wood cut and stacked."

"Can I give you a hand?" Fay asked Nemesio.

"No. The boys like to be lumbermen. They will be through in no time." Neither of the two men saw the look on the faces of the three lumbermen.

If Fay didn't have a pig of his own, he always bought the first one from Nemesio. Fay looked forward to the big day even though he did not understand what anyone said unless they spoke to him in English.

The 14th finally arrived. The Gods must have been at peace, since it was an especially nice day for December. Fay arrived early to help Nemesio with last minute preparations. About a half hour after Fay, the others started to arrive. Some brought a jug of *Vino Fino*, whiskey such as Old Grand Dad, a case of Olympia Beer, and even a jug of muscatel.

They gathered at the Barayasarra's house, which did not have drinkable running water. Good water came from the Byfield's well. Fay recruited his sons to bring water by the bucketful as needed throughout the day. Nemesio and Fay argued about paying the boys.

"No, you don't pay the boys."

"Oh, yes I do. As much water as they brought over, they worked hard and earned it. You betcha boots, they get paid."

"Thank you, Mr. Frank," from John.

"Thank you, Mr. Frank," from Bob.

Several pots of Hills Bros. Coffee, brewed sheepherder style, by adding the coffee grounds to the surface of the boiling water in the blue and white porcelain coffee pot, was consumed by the participants.

Each wife, in her fanciest apron, brought her favorite dish to ease Victorina's expenses and workload for two meals, which lately has been closer to three.

"Are we ready to slaughter our hogs? Finish your coffee and pass the jug around. Oh, everyone's finished? Good. Let's go." Nemesio was ready with his .22 rifle, box of shells, and two edged dagger. The other men picked up whatever else was needed. Down to the river they marched like the varsity team to a pep rally, all hyped up and ready for the next order from Nemesio. Instead, loud and clear from above, seemed to come, "YOU LIKA ME, I LIKA YOU. YOU NO LIKA ME, I NO LIKA YOU!" Through laughter some tried to say, "Nemesio, you've been replaced this year."

The scalding tank, a rectangular, welded iron structure 4x8x2 feet deep, was positioned over a trench three feet deep and three feet across and open at each end to feed the fire. On each long side, flush with the top of the tank, Nemesio built platforms made with 2x6s with enough dirt between platform and fire to keep the platform from burning. Even at that, an occasional bucket of river water was needed.

The water was near scalding hot because Fay started it when he noticed no one had. If he hadn't declined the invitation for coffee, it would have caused a delay. From Nemesio, Fay is honored, "Thank you, Fay—you saved our day. Give this man a drink." Nemesio loads the .22 and gives the command, "Let's get a pig—Fay's pig."

Nemesio determined the order in which the pigs were killed, shot the pig, plunged the dagger into its heart, gutted the animal, and oversaw the entire operation. This was okay with the others as it allowed them to visit. Actually, there was plenty to do for all.

The men were happy the pens were cleared of pig shit and a layer of straw scattered over the area. A "V-formation" was in place. The pig was chased into the narrow end. Nemesio aimed and pulled the trigger, WHACK, a perfect shot. The rifle was handed to Fay. Four men rushed in and grabbed a leg of the pig to hold it still. Fay handed Nemesio the dagger which he plunged into the pig's heart. Someone else caught the blood in a galvanized bucket which was then given to Frank or Jimmy to stir in a precise amount of salt so the blood would not clot. Later, this blood would be prepared with leek, onions, garlic, or whatever and stuffed into the clean intestines as a Basque blood sausage.

The pig was then carried, in a wheelbarrow, to the scalding tank. Four men each grabbed a leg and swung the pig back and forth to get enough momentum.

"Okay, men, on the count of three: One. Two. Three." The pig made a perfect landing on the wire netting spread on one of the platforms. Two men on the opposite platform were handed their pole nailed to the wire netting. The four men rocked the pig back and forth in the hot water until the bristles were soft enough to be scraped off.

If soft enough, the men on one side passed their pole to the other side and four or so men pulled the pig out of the tank and began scraping the softened bristles off. Louie was one of the scrapers.

Nemesio and some of the men went back to the pig pen for the next hog. "That one, Faustino's pig." The selected hog was chased into the narrow end of the V and the same procedure as before was followed.

Fay's hog was ready to be gutted while Faustino's was ready to be scalded. Gutting took place on an old willow tree which was equipped with several pulley systems. Nemesio cut slits behind the Achilles tendon to hang the carcass upside down.

Nemesio cut around the anus and the slit was started down the belly side of the hog. When he reached the anterior end of the abdomen, he collected the contents in a washtub.

"I'll take my liver and heart, Frank, but you can have the blood and intestines. Gertrude says someday she will learn how to make chorizos, but now I can't use them."

"Thank you, Fay. I'll send you some."

"I'll take these home right now. I'll be right back after I get a few chores done."

"See you later. And thanks, again, for getting the water heated. Hey, boys, come here. The first tub of guts is ready. I've separated the guts from the rest of the junk. Turn the intestines inside out like I showed you. Do you remember how?" He spoke in Euskara to them as he always did.

"Yes," Jimmy answers in English.

"Yes," Frank answers in English. (Both parents spoke to the children in Euskara. The children answered Dad in English and Mom in Euskara.)

The boys carried the tub of guts to the edge of the river next to the plank which jutted out over the water. Each took a length of intestine, folded one end inside out, and blew into the fold so a little pouch of air was formed. This was quickly dipped into the river to replace the air. More and more water was added, causing the intestine to turn inside out. Once inside out, the intestine was squeezed between the thumb and index so that the contents were removed. The intestine was put in a bucket to be cleaned better at a later time.

The boys made a game of the task. They tried to be the first to notice the other put the intestine too close to his lips when he blew the air bubble into the fold.

"Hey, dork, you have pig poop around your mouth."

"Well, so do you."

"You lika me, I lika you," one would start.

"You no lika me, I no lika you," the other finished.

At any lull in the flow of pig guts, they sneaked to the whiskey bottle and took a swig. When they were noticed, the whiskey found a new home. As they received the last pig's intestine, Frank asked, "Where did they hide the whiskey?"

"I dunno. Maybe they drank it all," Jimmy replied.

"Hell, if they drank it all, everyone would be singing, 'If you lika me, I lika you'—not just Faustino."

Nemesio, Fay and two others took their pigs with them while three came back the next day to get theirs.

"Hey, Frank. You know, tomorrow what I am going to miss? 'You lika me.'"

"Yeah."

Episode 36

Castration and Docking of Lambs
for Dummies

"Na—egh! No one does that. Or ever did. What kind of idiot do you take me for to believe something like that? Have you ever bit the nuts off a lamb? Or helped, or even watched anyone do it?"

"Wait up a bit! I didn't say people. Let me answer some of your questions. First off, oh yes, some people did and probably still do castrate lambs in this way even if other ways are available. No, they don't run alongside of them, biting up at the nuts. I didn't say they bite them off. My teeth have never been used."

My brother and I would catch the lamb for dad to do the castrating. With our right hand we held the lamb's right hind leg and the lamb's right front leg together, doing the same with the left legs. The rump of the lamb was placed on a platform, with the rear of the lamb facing Dad and the scrotum upwards. Dad would grab the scrotum with his left hand and cut the tip of the scrotum off with the knife in his right hand. Now all hands are doing something. The nuts are sticking out the cut end of the scrotum. With his teeth he would hold on to one testis and pull it up while scraping the sperm cord with the knife. He then dropped the nut in a pail—the same thing with the second nut. Then the tail would be cut off. All that for the males. Females only went through docking, getting their tails cut off.

Some answers: First, why do pictures of sheep in the Bible have long tails? If the tails are not cut off, that is what sheep look like. Why then are the lambs docked? Wool grows on tails and tails grow near the *kakaleku* and if the sheep get the runs and if flies lay eggs they become maggots and the burrow into the flesh of the lamb and that sure as hell ain't good. No tail means less wool to soak up *kaka* and less chance for maggots.

"Okay that makes sense so off with the tails. But the nuts?" If they did use teeth and all that, it must hurt the lamb like hell and I can't imagine what it is like for the owner of the teeth—so why do it?

Let's start with saving them in the bucket. They are cleaned up and cooked with scrambled eggs and cook up grey gobs in yellow eggs. I thought they looked like snot and as a brat kid, I did not eat them. Maybe now as an old man brat, I probably would try them.

There are at least three reasons. First, the boy lambs would fool around with the girl lambs and they don't go to confession.

Second. The female animal's meat tastes better than the male. Castrating doesn't change the male into a female but it removes the chief source of testosterone and therefore the meat will be less male-like.

The third reason is the strongest. About 40 percent of sheep carry a lethal recessive gene. Recessive means it needs to inherit two genes, one from each parent, to be expressed. Lethal means it will not live. Forty percent is a very high number. It can be controlled by using a buck that is not a carrier. The worst the lambs from this buck can be is a carrier lamb, which is as healthy as any. However if the buck is a carrier and the ewe also is a carrier, a lethal lamb can be produced. And that is why lambs are castrated.

Episode 37

A Penny Saved is Five Dollars is a Cow Bred

"Come on Boys, we need to help Ezra," Dad drops that on Frank and me after breakfast one brisk September morning. The Ezra needing help was a Holstein bull calf named after Ezra Taft Bensen, the U.S. Secretary of Agriculture during President Eisenhower's term, and later to become President of the Mormon Church. Lest you get the wrong idea why a cute Holstein bull calf would honor a member of the L.D.S. Church, it was not because we were devout or even Jack Mormons, because we were neither. Mormonism had nothing to do with Dad's baptismal practice of young bull calves. Dad, not being a Republican, had everything to do with it, plus it was not an honor to be so named.

A bull serves a purpose on a dairy farm—to breed the cows, as needed, and that is all. He gives no milk, eats a lot of hay, and gets big, mean, and dangerous to handle. Therefore, Dad tried to arrange events so that most, if not all the cows were bred. He would sell the bull and go bull-less as long as possible. If a cow came into heat during these times, he used a neighbor's bull. If no one had a bull at the time, he paid five dollars to have a breeding service bring a bull to the farm when the cow was in heat.

Ezra was a bull calf being raised to become the next resident breeding bull. So what was Ezra's problem and just what could Dad, Frank, and I do to help? Calling Ezra a calf was about as accurate as one could get. Ezra was still being fed milk and yet when the cow came into heat, he knew what to do, except, "*kakalekua baihu dekusu*" (His asshole was too low.) This equates to telling our kids to be patient; they aren't old enough; their time will come.

How did Dad organize the data to come up with his solution to the problem at hand? (1) one cow in heat, (2) no bull to breed her, (3) bull calf eagerly volunteers, (4) critical equipment does not make correct alignment, (5) female is too high, (6) male too low, (7) ah ha! solution obvious, (8) lower female-digging, and (9) raise male—heaping.

Frank held onto the halter. Dad alongside kept the excited cow in hole on one side, and I did the same on the other side. Ezra seemed to know his duties and was not at all bashful.

"Almost there, boys," Dad said as if the two of us were as excited as Ezra. "Pull the cow out.

One more time. Jimmy, get on the mound."

"What? He doesn't mean for me to ..."

"Tramp on that dirt ..."

"Whew!"

The cow was pushed into the hole. Frank had the halter, Dad and me, at the sides again. The cow's udder was below ground-level.

Ezra came running with the enthusiasm of the entire LDS membership. He approached in slow motion, soared through the heavens, and made a perfect ejaculation with seagulls watching.

"See, boys, we saved five dollars."

Episode 38
The Barayasarra Boys: A#1 Haystackers

Nemesio was the undisputed loose hay stacking champion of the Grand View Valley—a point not likely to be challenged in his day or for years thereafter. This type record tends to fade as memories do and as record holders die off. And to start with, does anyone care? I do.

Nemesio's hay stacks were the tallest and straightest of any of the neighboring farms, monuments to be marveled at in their own right. The tops had to be rounded in the most perfect of geometric domes— and not a single strand of hay was allowed to litter the ground around the base of the stack. Had this man had the educational opportunities, would this talent and efforts be seen in buildings and bridges? This avenue of perfectionism on his part was not because the sheep or cow might prefer their hay come from such a beautiful stack. This avenue of perfectionism in using hay rather than marble did not result from competition from any neighbor, as it did not.

"Your Old Man is a compulsive perfectionist!" Basillio told us repeatedly. "Look at that stack—three miles high and straighter than his nose!"

That reference or any other to Nemesio's nose did not make me comfortable. After all, it did stick out there a ways and everybody told me again and again, "You have your dad's nose!"

Whatever he may have had that I wanted to inherit from him, it certainly was not that nose.

As the switch was finally made from loose to baled hay, this compulsion stayed with him. Since hay bales are not uniform in length and compactness, he picked 'just the right one' for the moment. Bales used on the edge of the stack had to be neatly cut, and even interior bales had to fit just so. At times he would leave a spot open to see if a better bale might come up on the next load.

It was never a matter of dispute who was to stack, even with a neighbor's hay. At times as the stack began to reach and disappear into the heavens, the neighbor was prone to say, "That's high enough Frank."

"We can put the rest of your hay up here. That way, you don't have to move the derrick and start a new butt."

"No, that's high enough! I don't like to climb up there when I need to use the hay if it's too high."

"Well, I do need a load or two to finish it off."

And about six or seven loads later, he would concede and come down to start a new butt. The stack was always a dozen or so more than the neighbor wanted and twenty or so less than Nemesio's idea.

Whenever the stack was higher than the neighbor wanted, Nemesio did not hesitate to "start" or to "open" the stack for him. Opening a stack involved climbing to the top and pitching off some of the hay and/or cutting steps with a hay knife.

Grand View Farms, formally known as The Bruneau Sheep Company, hired son, Louis, as a stacker of baled hay who carried on and added to the Barayasarra reputation. Unlike Nemesio's method, Grand View Farms used a uniform system: Each butt was six by seven bales and was fourteen bales high. Each row of bales followed a certain pattern which kicked in with the third row—single row of bales on outside, then a double row, then butts out with pattern repeating. The advantage of the "system" was that the placement of bales was automatic and it was easier to estimate number and/or tonnage of hay by counting butts.

Frank and I followed Lou. Actually my first summer job at Grand View Farms was a "baler chaser" who forks over broken bales and bits of hay the baler missed into rows the baler is on. I followed Lou's advice to the letter. "Always be busy: Don't just sit around no matter how tired you are or how little there is to do at the moment. You are not being paid $7.00 a day to sit on your ass." The so-called Protestant work ethic was alive with this Catholic family.

The Barayasarra hay stacking dynasty was to end abruptly with twentieth century technology. Frank and I were the last, replaced by hay stacking machines. Neither of us ever learned how to harness a horse.

Mike never worked at Grand View Farms. It was hard to see this art lost and the Mormon derrick die such a neglected death.

Yes, it was time to quit the day job and venture into new careers—maybe teaching.

Episode 39
Nobody Goes Out on Halloween Night
from My House
Part 1: Original Degree

"No one from MY house is going out to tip over out-houses on Halloween night or on any other night. That is the dumbest thing I ever heard! Last year someone was in his when someone pushed it over, and he almost died—wasn't found until the next morning. And you have the nerve to ask if you can go!" That was that and Mom settled it with Louie. Louie went out in the yard to cool off. (Keep that in mind as I continue.)

Meanwhile let us look at the drama I was having with Felipa at the time. I was having a fit. She made me some cocoa—how nice of her. Hold on! Since we had no refrigerator, we boiled our milk to pasteurize it. This caused the milk to form a skin on the surface, which I did not like. Apparently, Felipa boiled the milk so the cocoa had a skin on the surface. I was not at all happy and was near meltdown. I carried my protest to my bed, demanding reasonably and as diplomatically as I could that she make me a new cup of cocoa. She wasn't moving.

I caved. Besides she or Mom is apt to pour it down the sink and then what—nothing! I stepped off the bed. Something grabbed my ankle. "YEEOW! Let me go LET GO! YEOWW!" Something was under the bed. I was really screaming because something grabbed my leg. Before it was fake screaming—well, o.k. it was spoiled brat screaming.

Even Dad came in. "Look!" he said holding the bed covers up, "There is nothing under the bed! NOTHING! LOOK!"

I looked. "There. . ." There was nothing "But. It grabbed my ankle." After that, I was afraid to get into bed—I jumped from about three feet away.

About three months later, Lou said, "There is nothing under the bed. There never was."

"You don't know. You weren't there—I was. Something grabbed my leg." I said.

"I was there."

"Where?"

"Under the bed."

"I looked—you weren't,"

"I came through the window, crawled under the bed, grabbed your ankle, crawled out, went out the window, and followed right behind Dad. Best Halloween I ever had."

"You asshole."

Episode 39
Nobody Goes Out on Halloween Night
from My House
Part 2: The Loophole

A few years past the there-is-something-under-the-bed-Halloween, Louie was attending Oklahoma City University. Mom's Papal Decree was still in effect as the eleventh commandment but now had the support of tradition. The same Congress which passes laws, for all of us to follow, gave us the loophole. When I became old enough for the decree to be in effect, there was a loophole—Dad was going to town to play Nine-Card-Rummy. Since he was going, I was allowed to go but I had better not touch a single outhouse.

I kept my word. I didn't even go near one. Instead, we went to Bruneau to do our stuff. The sheriff of Owyhee County had an old flatbed pickup, which he drove during his off hours. He had to "pop the clutch" to get it started. To do so, he parked at the top of a slight incline, got the vehicle to rolling, jumped in, and popped the clutch. Normally a single person can do it. There were four of us. So if a drunk sheriff could do it alone, four healthy boys should have no problem. If the one to do the actual clutch popping had not tried to help with the pushing, it would have worked. Just as he was to jump in, he slipped and the truck got away from us.

The truck slowly rolled down the hill, off the road at the bottom, up a dry irrigation canal bank, and into it. Even though no damage was done, the prank was a little more than any of us anticipated.

What to do? What to do? Should we go in and confess to the law? Then I had an idea, "Let's just say we saw some other kids do it."

"No. The police get you in a room by yourself and torture you until you confess," was the response. We did the honorable thing—nothing. "Just don't say anything to anyone at school or each other, or even home." We went back to Grand View after our life of crime. My idea was that police always get the guilty. The sheriff was so drunk, he confessed and resigned.

This guilt was too much for me, so I asked my mother, "Will I see Mr. Pinder?"

"No, you just had your hair cut last week."

"No, his other job."

"Bartending?"

"No, at the state pen?"

"Why would you need to see him at the pen?"

"Pushing the sheriff's truck in the canal. Mama, I didn't mean to. It got away from us."

"When did you do that?"

"Last night. Halloween night."

"You did no such thing. Two old ladies saw him drive his truck into the canal. He was passed out when they checked on him. That was three days ago. Yesterday he resigned. Last night you had one of your nightmares. You yelled and screamed, one of your worst in a long time."

"Oh Mama, it was horrible."

Episode 40

Geometry, Brains, and Help

Mr. Riddlemoser, Meridian High School Principal, was also the teacher for one section of geometry in which I was enrolled along with four or five of the *better-than-you-are-so-my-poop-doesn't-smell* popular girls. I didn't know any of them and they didn't know me. They kept "psst, Charlie" all period long. I ignored them because I wasn't Charlie.

The test consisted of four proofs to work out. This was before computers so the tests were copied on mimeograph machines. I sailed through the first three problems but my fourth one was printed with a big fold through it. I went up to get a good copy and yes, I left my completed problems on my desk, and yes, it was gone. So I worked out the last proof with ten minutes left, no paper came backed. I reworked the three easily.

At the bell, "Pass your papers in."

I passed my second copy in with all four problems finished. I was confident of a 100%. My original they passed to me at the bell, I stuck in my geometry book. At home, I looked at my paper and my lovely friends made changes. They were sure they would get 75% and I would only get 25%. I never told them I didn't pass in the paper they returned.

Later in the year, one of the girls asked for proper help, which I did give. "Thank you, Charlie," she said.

"No problem," I answered.

Episode 41
Will the NBA Draft Jimmy?

Grand View High School was as small as one would expect for graduates of a two-room grade school. Not only was it expected that all boys went out for sports, it was expected they go out for all sports. This included basketball, baseball, and track. The school did not have enough males for football and could not afford tennis courts. Wrestling had not yet made its way as a high school sport.

Louis was a good athlete—consistently high scorer on the basketball team, catcher for the baseball team, and very competitive in track. This added to my anxiety—not only were all males expected to participate in all sports, but my brother set an impossible precedent for me to meet.

During my eighth grade year, the seventh and eighth graders were moved from the tworoom grade school to one of the rooms in the high school. This was great. We were now "Big Shots" and away from the little children. And, best of all, if our grades were high enough, we could take typing with the high school students if there were open typewriters available. What more could one ask?

Well, there was one drawback at least for me: we were thrust into athletics a year earlier. My classmates looked forward to this aspect but not me. I felt very inadequate in this area.

During basketball games, since small schools did not have a Junior Varsity team, the high school girls played the first game—that is, if the opposing school had a girls' team. If not, someone decided that our seventh and eighth grade boys could play the high school girls with one-half of the game using boys' rules and the other half using girls' rules. This was fine if we won, but not so if we lost to girls—even if they were older than us.

In those days, girls' basketball was a different game from the boys. Each team had six, not five, members—three guards and three forwards. Guards had to stay on the half of the floor with the opponent's basket and the forwards stayed on the half with their basket and the opponent's guards. Only one dribble was allowed and the ball had to be passed to someone else.

What do girls' rules have to do with my career in basketball? Nothing, except that this was the seventh and eighth grade boys' ticket to "big time" ball before they started high school.

The gymnasium, which also served as auditorium, had a stage at one end over the locker rooms and the entrance was immediately under the basket at the other end. Above the basket was an open balcony which opened into a large room, also serving as a class room since the seventh and eighth graders were now occupying one of the regular classrooms. This was the only room on the second floor and was open during basketball games so that spectators could watch the game from the balcony level.

We were playing the girls during the boys' rules half of the game. I stole the ball and was dribbling alone toward our basket under the balcony. Notwithstanding my vertical jump of six inches, it was a sure two-pointer. Just as I was about to shoot, Larry Uriona, a family friend and alumnus of GVHS, gave me a supporting root.

"Come on, Jimmy!"

I never knew what it was about Larry's presence that intimidated me. I liked and admired him very much and especially did not want to screw up in his presence. As I started up, I heard him. I not only missed the shot, I missed the backboard, shooting the ball over it and into the balcony. I continued right out the door into the hallway. Everyone thought I went to retrieve the ball.

I did not. I went home. Humiliated, I didn't bother to change clothes. The weekend was horrible as I anticipated the reaction and remarks I would get at school. This was a secondary problem. At the moment, I could not return in my disgrace before my fellow teammates, students, spectators, and Larry Uriona. I have no memory of what happened at school the following Monday—a convenient memory block, I'm sure.

Well, so much for basketball. Shall we try track?

There were three of us eighth grade boys who participated in some of the track contests. In running high jump, Richard Beal was by far the best and Ivan Arnold and I were about the same— some days I out jumped him and on other days, he out jumped me. A meet was scheduled on a nice May afternoon with Bruneau, our arch rival school. We looked forward to the event and when the day finally arrived, we were surprised and pleased to learn that Bruneau had no real competitors. Since a blue ribbon was first place, red second, and white third, the prospects of my receiving no ribbon at all became a chance for the second place red, if I could out-do Ivan.

Richard, a shoe-in for first, became overconfident, began to show off, and messed up. The impossible occurred; the prospects now included a chance for First Place Blue Ribbon—from no ribbon to blue. There must be a God.

My adrenaline was working but so was Ivan's. We were both jumping better than ever— even out-jumping Richard's practice jumps. The officials kept raising the pole, an inch at a time.

I got set; I took off. About four feet from the pole, getting ready to soar over the moon, I heard it. "Come on Jimmy!" Larry had joined the crowd.

Forget the moon. Forget the jump. I did. I ran through knocking the pole off. My second try was uninspiring since my concentration was now broken. Ribbons were awarded: Richard did not stay to receive his white. I received red. Ivan, blue.

My Olympic prospects dimmed, the world would have to wait for someone else to jump over the moon.

Episode 42

If Guns Don't Kill People,
What About Brooms?

What did the few Basque families in Grand View do for entertainment? They visited each other. The visits were unannounced since there were no telephones in the entire Grand View valley. The visits were pleasant and were a means of getting news about other Basques or to organize attendance and rides for funerals. As children, we enjoyed some visits more than others: Favorites were Basilio and Briqueta of Mountain Home who not only brought treats but liked to play tricks on us. Least favorite was the lady who dunked my head in the river.

One of the frequent visitors were Felipa and John Uriona, parents of Larry whom I have included in another story.

They came down one summer evening with daughter, Sophia, who was a schoolmate of Louie. They were visiting on the front step and of course, I was out there as well—after all why wouldn't I be welcome?

"I have the car keys and the folks will be visiting for a couple of hours more, let's go up town and see if anything is happening. Do you want to go?" Sophie asks.

"Sure. Let's go."

We, the three, start for the car. "Oh not you, Jimmy, your *kakaleku* is too low—go pee in the stove."

"No, you're not going. Go back," Louie seconds the demand.

"I get the picture. I know when I'm not wanted. You only need say so once," I said as I went back to the house and they left in Uriona's car. Then inside with as much revenge as I had, "Louie and Sophie went up town." Dad and John continued visiting while the two moms went outside.

They watched the taillights going south between our place and Byfields, turn east between our place and Totoricas, then north to Grand View.

They watched every set of headlights on the road and finally a car made the appropriate turns. Then the lights went out near Totoricas. A little past the time the lights went out the presumed sinners showed up.

"*Jesus, Maria, eta Jose.*" With the help of the Holy Family, Mrs. Uriona brought the broom down on Louie's head, "Not with my daughter!" John came out to de-broom his wife.

"We didn't do anything, we played pool."

"Don't tell me that. I wasn't born yesterday morning. I saw the lights go out on the car."

Sophie comes up with: "I turned them off. We drove in the dark."

"Why? You can do better than that."

"So you wouldn't see we were gone."

The constitution does not say one thing about the right of one to turn lights off. However, The National Broom Association claims the second amendment gives mothers the right to hit a male over head with a broom if she wasn't born yesterday morning.

Episode 43

To the Doctor with Jose Totorica

It was early fall 1946 and brother Louis was not feeling well at all. He was completely exhausted with muscles and joints in unbearable pain. Measles like blotches covered his body. To confuse matters further, he had recently gone to a dentist to have a tooth extracted. The first dentist refused. The second dentist extracted the tooth with no questions asked. So was his infection caused by the tooth which should not have been extracted? Was it Rocky Mountain Spotted Fever? Or was it Rheumatic Fever? The one doctor serving Mountain Home and Grand View was puzzled.

Louie was to be admitted to a hospital in Boise as soon as he could get there, some sixty miles of partially paved, partially unpaved dirt road away. Unfortunately there was no ambulance service available at the time.

Some other way had to be found by the family to get Louie to more qualified medical care.

Nemesio was not familiar with driving in the "big" city of Boise. Grand View was one thing but transporting a sick child to a hospital in an unfamiliar place was quite another. If this weren't such a serious life or death situation, he would have uttered his remark by now, "Your uterus will come out before I do this for you again."

Anyway Jose Totorica, Basque neighbor, whose farm touched ours on the south side, did the driving. Jose was a pleasant soul, always in overalls and always with a lovely smile, a twinkle in his eye, and a most engaging laugh, "hehehehe." Sometimes his sentences and his laugh combined and trailed off together.

"Jesus Christ, Jose. Slow down! The goddamn speed limit is about half the speed you're going! We're all going to die right here if you don't slow down!"

"Hehehehe. Speed limits don't count when you have to get a sick child to the doctor. To the hospital! They don't tell you to get to the hospital in a month or two. I have never heard a doctor say anything about speed limits. They mean, now. NOW, hehehehe."

Half the time Dad had his foot on the passenger side brake, and prayed the other half religiously with his eyes closed.

"Jose. You went through a stop sign? *Dios*! Have you gone mad? *Hostia*."

"When it's an emergency, you have to get there one way or the other—and in a hurry. You fine, Louie hehehehe!"

"Keep your eyes on the road, Jose! I'll, take care of Louie—and the shit in my pants, *también*."

"Hehehehe. I'll get Louie to the hospital. But Nemesio, you will have to take care of the shit on your own hehehehe,"

The entire trip went like that: Nemesio complained and Jose ignored him. Finally, they pulled into the emergency entrance. The hospital took Louie off in a wheelchair. "Go with Louie. I'll park the car and meet you at the room."

"Thank you Jose. You did a wonderful job."

"Hehehehe." The two checked Louis in and visited a few minutes. The ride home was more relaxed for Nemesio.

Nemesio was very thankful of Jose's generosity and was concerned that he was too negative, "Thank you my friend. You have more balls than I do—I couldn't have made the trip."

"Anytime, Nemesio. Hehehehe."

Louie stayed in the hospital a week and received the wonder drug, penicillin, for rheumatic fever and an enlarged heart. He would be bedridden for five months. Felipa brought his assignments to him from school and he taught himself the material and graduated with a straight A average, not only high school but first grade through high school.

One day I came home from school—well, I came home every day from school, but that day, I had special news to share with my alpha brother. I rushed to his bedside. "Guess what I heard in school today?" No enthusiastic response, so I told him anyway, "Shirley Smith had rheumatic fever and had to stay in bed a whole year."

A fist came from nowhere, under the covers, I assume. My chin hit that fist as hard as I could, so hard that the floor came up and hit my ass. I left quietly to explain to Mom what Louie did, "for no reason at all. I'm not going to tell him anything."

"Thank God for that!" from Lou's bedroom.

Sometime after the Totoricas left Grand View and moved to Boise, Jose was in a car-train accident and passed from this life. He is remembered.

Episode 44

Inviting the School Principal
to a Basque Dinner

Education and teachers were held with utmost respect by Nemesio and Victorina. Whatever the teacher said, it was never to be questioned. If one of the children came home from school with a complaint concerning something a teacher did or said, the response was always:

"And just what did you do to cause it? Don't tell me what they did—tell me what you did!"

A report that you were punished at school automatically meant you were again punished at home—no questions asked. By the time we children were in high school, we learned not to complain at home. In fact, we considered it to be an embarrassment if a student's parent visited school; the student was viewed as pathetic and weak if this happened, especially if a mother arrived at school. As adults, this attitude taught them (1) to realize the world was not always fair, and (2) how to handle one's own problems independently.

During Louie's senior year, it was decided that the Grand View High School principal, Mr. Jim Morris, would be invited to a home cooked Basque dinner. Victorina was an extremely good cook and was known to prepare a meal on such occasions with several choices of meats and fish as well as several side dishes of vegetables and desserts. She would also include several American choices just in case the guest was not used to the spices and garlic of Basque food. Considering the extreme poverty of the family, it was no easy task, especially considering Victorina's perfectionism. Usually after such a meal, when everyone had eaten much too much, she would look at the amount of food left over and wonder, "Did they enjoy it? Probably not since so little was eaten."

The date was set, Mr. Morris was invited, and word was sent back that he would attend. Jim and Frank were as excited as anyone since these occasions were a rare respite from the usual menu of beans and potatoes. Victorina was busy with Felipa's help—after all, Mr. Morris was her principal, too. The house had to be spotless and several of the dishes required preparations measured in days rather than minutes or hours.

The date finally arrived and the event went off without a hitch, even with much of the conversation involving Lou and Felipa acting as interpreters between principal and mother. By this time, Nemesio felt comfortable enough with English to speak directly to the guest of honor. Victorina was in charge of every detail, making sure that each course was served at the appropriate time. She never ate with the guests, insisting she gets plenty to eat.

After the meal, the table was cleared and prepared for the visiting which would take place around it. Felipa helped her mother with the clearing of the table and the washing of the dishes.

Jim Morris was impressed and during the course of the visiting, thanked Victorina, Nemesio, Lou, Felipa, and whoever else was around again and again. Nemesio excused himself to make sure the livestock was fed and watered.

Mr. Morris and Lou continued to visit for a few minutes until it was time for Mr. Morris to leave. Mr. Morris, as a special gesture to Victorina, thought it would be especially touching if he could thank her in Euskara and tell her what a good time he had. He asked Lou to coach him in this detail. He repeated it over and over to Lou, with the student now taking the role of teacher and teacher that of student. Finally, he and Lou were satisfied that he could remember all the words and had the accent down properly.

Mr. Morris got up, went over to the sink where Victorina was washing dishes, put his arm around her shoulder, and with perfect expression and accent said, "*Eskerrik asko, hatuek, kakan gustue okedo.*" "Thank you very much, the food tasted like shit!")

Victorina screamed, "Louie!" and went after him. Felipa, Jimmy, and Frank rolled with laughter and glee. Lou, pleased with himself, was out in the yard and out of harm's way.

And Jim Morris, realizing that a practical joke had been played on him, went from one child to another asking, "What did I say? What did your brother have me say?" Of course, no one would tell him. You just didn't use such words with a teacher, let alone a high school principal. Victorina did her best, with her limited English, to assure him it was okay, that it was Lou's joke. It was years after Lou's graduation that he would finally tell him.

Episode 45

High School: A Moment of Pride

It was May 1947, and Louis, the firstborn, was graduating from Grand View High School. Although Nemesio was not prone to expressing his feelings, he was a very proud man that evening. Victorina was not at all ashamed to show her feelings. After all, she had the equivalent of an eighth grade education while Nemesio claimed six years, which she insisted, was closer to three.

"And he played hooky half of those years," she would add to her first correction.

"And why should I go to school? To get my knuckles rapped by the teacher with a ruler?" would be his counter.

Both were very intelligent and supported the idea of a good education, especially Victorina. She had to stay home as the eldest daughter of eight children to help with the babysitting of her siblings. Nemesio, although not much for school, was a self-taught man. He taught himself to read and do math and would delight in working out long division problems faster than his children who had more formal schooling than he.

Thus, it was understandable that a good amount of pride would show through on this graduation day. Not only was Lou, the first in the Barayasarra lineage, graduating from high school, he was the class valedictorian with a straight "A" average. He out-performed all the Red Hairs and that was a precious feeling to the family.

Victorina seldom went anywhere. Hiring baby sitters was never considered, and the few times someone helped out with the children, Victorina was giving birth to a child or very ill.

She owned one dress, polka dotted, several years old, for these rare occasions. Besides getting herself ready, she had to lay out clothes for five children and oversee their preparations.

Baths were taken, serial fashion in the same water, in an old washtub filled with Snake River water heated on the coal stove. Nemesio's one suit had to be dry-cleaned by hand and aired out for the event. Nemesio would complain about the amount of time she was taking to get ready and this would add to the anxiety of the moment. It was an understatement to say that the event had to be important for Victorina to leave the house.

This was one of those occasions. The family sat in the high school gymnasium/auditorium with Lou sitting on the stage with the other graduates. They listened as Lou delivered the valedictory address, punctuated with proper remarks of patriotism, thank you to parents, teachers, etc. It was indeed a precious moment for the family, and sister Felipa would be repeating the process as valedictorian the next year.

However, it was not unexpected that the few scholarships went to the other less worthy classmates. Lou knew, and the family knew, that they would go to the Red Hairs with the "B" averages. "After all, the Barayasarras are too poor to take advantage of these scholarships. They would not be able to pay the other costs beyond the tuition award, so why waste them?" was the justification.

Yet, the family was proud—Louie had outperformed those Red Hairs who would go on to college. Since the awarding of the scholarships was expected, the satisfaction of beating them academically was reward enough at the moment.

As the family and friends filed out at the end of the ceremony, Victorina was joined by Felipa Uriona and the two ladies began to visit in their native Euskara. "Your Louie did a fine job!

Yes, very fine."

"Thank you, he worked very hard and was always good with books."

About that time, Tom Brown (not his real name), President of the School Board and next door neighbor to the Uriona farm, passed the ladies. "Speak English, ladies! This is America and we speak English here," came his intimidating demand.

Shocked and embarrassed, the two women immediately stopped visiting. However, Larry, Felipa's oldest son, in his twenties, was not about to let this insult of Victorina and his own mother go unchallenged. He grabbed Tom by the lapel of his suit and brought his other closed fist across

Tom's jaw. Tom ended up on the floor with a broken nose and bloodied face.

"I caused this—with my two words in Euskara," Victorina lamented.

"No, that idiot was the cause. Don't you feel bad," Felipa assured her. "Now you see what we put up with all the time with him as our neighbor. And our Larry just can't let things like that pass."

"Just so they don't take away Louie's diploma. That Red Hair is on the School Board, you know!"

"That won't happen. Don't worry!"

But worry Victorina did—and if she seldom ventured out of the house before, she did so less after that night. If asked to go anywhere other than visits to the Urionas or Guisasolas, she would always respond, "And what happened the one time I did? Two grown men fighting like children. And over what? That I spoke two words in Euskara to Felipa Uriona. No thank you."

"Besides, my polka dot dress will last forever, if I don't go anywhere."

But she did attend each of her children's high school graduations.

Episode 46

Byfield's Watermelon: Father Forgive Me

"Don't talk to strangers," and "Never trust a 'Red Hair,'" were decrees my siblings and I were taught religiously by our parents—and understandingly so. It was a hostile world, Nemesio and Victorina taught their children. Nemesio was shot at during his herding days, and Victorina and the children were given a poisoned cake by a cowboy bearing his "welcome wagon gift." At school, they were called "Black Bascos" or were told to go back where they came from. The Ku Klux Klan, or just the fear of the Klan, was also a force foreigners had to deal with, as did our family. The hostility even went so far as Red Hairs not wanting their daughters to date and marry a Black Basco.

But even under such circumstances, the family had to trust some Red Hairs as all were not bad or hostile or unfair or unkind: some were good, friendly, fair, kind people. When such people were found, my family formed a mutualistic bond—they helped us and my generous dad would return the favor by sending a front quarter of a butchered lamb or produce from the ridiculously large weed-less garden he grew.

Such people included the Byfields, Fay and Gertrude, and their sons, Jonathan and Robert, who lived on the farm next to us, as well as Sam Mulinex, insurance salesman and self-appointed mayor. Any legal work or forms were taken to either Gertrude or Sam for help and advice.

Well, I have established that the Byfields were very good people and very important to the Barayasarra household, which makes my sin so far from a venial infraction that there may not be enough time in Purgatory to take care of it. What did I do? I'm getting there!

Fay also had a garden, but of course he didn't let a weed or two upset him. Along with lettuce, carrots, and rows and rows of cabbage, he planted several hills of watermelon, which soon lost the battle with weeds as pig weed and cheat grass camouflaged the melon plants except for one lone watermelon plant which seemed to be at peace with the weeds. Not only at peace, it had one lone watermelon, the biggest Fay had ever seen. Surprised and pleased, it was decided that the melon would be entered in the local county fair. He removed all the herbal competition from around the plant. Pleased with this new care, the melon responded by growing even bigger and nicer. It was a beauty.

Well, no surprises where this story is going. Yes, that is exactly what happened. We stole the goddamn melon—well, three of us were involved, but in the confessional I confess my sins only and in this account, I do the same. We took the melon to the riverbank and dropped it on a willow log and ate what we could of the pieces, throwing the rest into the river.

Did we get off scot-free? We didn't serve time and we weren't lynched, if that is what you mean. But, if there ever were a good example of Catholic guilt, that would be the best—or worst. Did we pay for this sin?—we certainly did, every minute since. If only I had a lamb to butcher, some unknown poor person would get a surprise—a front quarter.

Episode 47

The Byfields: Best Damn Red Hairs Around

Never trust strangers, especially if they are Red Hairs. The name Red Hair was what we Bascos called the non-Basque American, sort of our counterpart of Honky or Cracker, because so many were blondes or blondish. It was used toward all non-Basques, non-minority people, even if their hair was jet black. But once something becomes a rule, there are exceptions, and thus there were Red Hairs who were fantastic people. We grew up with a few, even in Grand View, Idaho. Two families who were the crème de la crème were the Sam Mullinex family and the Fay Byfield family.

Sam Mullinex was sort of a self-proclaimed mayor of the unincorporated three hundred or so Grand View area residents, although by profession he was probably an insurance agent. I suspect, at least with the few Basques, he fell into the mayoralty role, because he had to be the most educated person in town while still being a fair and compassionate individual.

But the family I want to write about is Fay and Gertrude Byfield and sons, Jonathan Rathbun Byfield, a few months older than I was, and Robert Fay Byfield, my brother Frank's age. Their combination of given and surnames should have made them suspect from the beginning. However, to us they were known as Fay, Mrs. Byfield, John, and Bob, a decent array of normal people names. It probably didn't hurt the relationship that they were as poor, if not more so, as we were.

They owned the bamboo fishing poles, but we owned the hook, which taught us valuable lessons in diplomacy at a very early age. After a disagreement, we would take our hook and they, their bamboo pole and fish line. The fact that neither could then fish was a perfect incentive to get negotiations back on track.

Dad would even the score by sending over vegetables from our garden or a front quarter of a freshly butchered lamb. During haying, we helped them with their crop and they helped us with ours.

They taught a stubborn old Basque about the value of a vet if a cow came down with milk fever (another story). Sometimes Dad and Fay argued—just like their kids. We had a Holstein cow in heat and Byfields, at that time, had a Holstein bull. Both sire and dam were black and white, the way God intended Holsteins to be. However, the calf born was a red and white bull calf and the two old men blamed the other's animal.

"Fay, it is your bull which isn't pure. That is an old, old cow and she has always had black and white calves."

"Not this time, you old goat, that calf looks red and white to me."

"Because of your bull, you stubborn old fart."

"No, your cow."

"Your bull."

It was too bad the matter wasn't as simple as fish hooks—the argument took longer than it took the Byfield and Barayasarra boys to settle the entire fishing rights of the Snake River.

Then it became time to go home, and Dad said, "What time do you want me to come over tomorrow to help with your hay, Fay?" I thought he was trying to be funny, and Fay should have said, "Anytime you're not a crank, Frank," but he didn't. Grownups are so dumb sometimes.

After Mrs. Byfield tried to teach a year, they sold their farm and moved to operate the Sunburst Hotel in Sunburst, Montana. We lost our best Red Hair friends the day they moved. I sure hope Dad didn't make them mad about that stupid red calf.

Episode 48
Cloudburst in Grand View
Part 1: It Rained

"The sun shines on the just and unjust alike"—words of wisdom not easily dismissed as a cliché—unless you want to battle *Matthew 5:45*. And of course it rains on both as well. Perhaps, the Prime Mover has His version of Creature Correctness in play. Maybe the Just-Unjust precedent is why sometimes evil happens to good creatures, so that perhaps *Isaiah 55* can be cited (out of context): "For my thoughts are not your thoughts, Nor are your ways my way..." Isn't that a tough one to swallow? But swallow it or not, accept it we must. We don't hold the patent or copyrights. (Never you mind, I – HAVE – NOT – BEEN –AROUND – LONG – ENOUGH – FOR – THEM – NOT – TO – APPLY!)

Well, enough of Theology 101 for now. Let those thoughts be background as I tell you about the cloudburst which fell on the just, the unjust, and my family sometime in the 1940s.

The bearded barley and unbearded oats, which grew together from seed Dad mixed before planting, looked nice as they were heading out. Grain fields weren't free from weeds then as they are today since chemical weed killers were yet to be produced. As the grain grew, so did the weeds— sunflowers, alkali weed, and morning glory. Those few areas with weeds too thick to thrash, Dad mowed for hay. Otherwise a binder cut and bound the stalks of grain, which were then propped upright into shocks to dry out and eventually haul to the stationary thrasher to separate grain from the straw.

It was one of those mornings when the just and unjust had a nice warm sunny day. The alfalfa fields looked nice and free from weeds and the grain fields waved their heads softly back and forth as if thankful to be so blessed and eager to return a bumper crop. Occasionally a dust bunny traveled down the dirt lanes to disappear as it traveled over a green alfalfa field in a breeze almost too calm to be noticed. At other times, the breeze picked up enough to be felt and enjoyed. The breeze was picking up speed moving toward the northeast while the western sky was clouding over. Quickly the blue sky was converting into a dark and stormy one.

"I don't like the looks of that," Nemesio says to no one, "it's changing too fast to be good." But not expecting it to last very long, he went to change the water set, not aware of the redundancy of his efforts.

A half hour later, the sky was as dark as a moonless night, the rain came down relentlessly pelting anyone and anything not protected, and lightning in all its fury burnt at the skies with tantrum flashes, letting the world know its mood.

Tootsie, an Australian sheep dog traumatized during her herding days by such a storm, was retired to life as a family pet. She was so shaggy that at times one had to note the direction she moved to determine which end to feed. Although an outside dog, she was allowed inside during thunder. She would get under the kitchen table, whimper, and shake. Frank and I would keep her company.

"Why did that man go out? He's seen a cloudburst or two to know when they are about to happen," Victorina pondered, returning to the rosary, "Holy Mary, Mother of God, Pray for us sinners, now and at the hour of our death."

By now, a flat, foot-deep river washed over the grain field, flattening the beautiful field of barley and oats, as it made its way to join the mighty Snake.

The storm stopped as suddenly as it began, and the sun began to quickly reclaim the heavens. The air smelled so clean and the birds chirped happily that the storm was over.

Mom paced back and forth along the yard fence facing the direction Nemesio had gone to change the water, but of course nothing was visible. She returned to the kitchen. This she did again and again, as she prayed decade after decade of the rosary.

As if in answer to her prayers, the storm stopped as quickly as it started—the sky cleared up, and looked cleansed. The sound of her prayers became one of thanksgiving with an element of concern for

Nemesio. The sky which just gave us the fear of hell now displayed a double rainbow of celestial love.

But where was Dad? He should have made it back by now. A sheet of water, about eight to twelve inches deep, flowed across our yard toward the river, flattening the beautiful grain field in its path. Then we heard it—a sound like an unhappy lost puppy would make, but not exactly. Tootsie recognized it as Nemesio and ran to meet him, followed by Mom and the two of us. Dad staggered up the walk, moving slowly, dragging one foot, then the other, falling now and then in the swift water at his feet. His big finger of his left hand was sideways in his mouth and he was trying to talk. All he could do were the child-like/animal-like sounds, as he tried to get his finger out of his mouth. We ran to help. As Mom touched his arm, his finger immediately was freed and he could talk and walk normally, albeit nervously and very weakly.

"I was making a change of water setting—I didn't expect this much rain. I took cover under a tree even though I know better but I didn't expect lightning to hit that particular tree. They say if you have something in your mouth, you will be okay. Well, I only had my finger. A big crack of lightning hit the tree. The next thing I remembered was being washed down the drain ditch toward the river. I managed to grab some willow saplings and pull myself out—all this with one hand. I couldn't get the other out of my mouth."

"Almost the same as what happened to my Elojio—my father. He was swept out to sea. His body was never found." She paused and then to either of us, "Get your Dad a clean glass of water and a cup of coffee," and then back to Dad, "Get out of those wet clothes and clean up a bit. Boys, get some warm water off the stove and get a bath ready for your dad. Use that tub by the door."

"Did you get the water changed?" She couldn't resist that one.

"Funny!"

Episode 48
Cloudburst in Grand View
Part 2: The Sun and Birds are Happy

Man too, can breathe the cleaned air although he had work to do to correct the damage.

Left by the brief but powerful storm. Sometimes the fury of such a storm is enough to put the comeback out of his range. He checks his losses along with areas where he was spared worse.

Once he checked his losses and did what he could, he, the Nemesios of the world, will check on others.

When he came in, Victorina asked him, "Do you feel okay? You had quite a shock."

"Yes, okay now. Why do you ask?"

"The last one of these was worse for Emetedio than us, when the canal broke at their place and flooded their house and cellar."

"You think we should check on them? I wondered the same thing." We drove to their place.

The flooding over the canal left a layer of mud in their house and yard.

"Be careful—the flood may have washed rattlesnakes down."

She served sandwiches but Frank and I didn't eat any because Frank said, "She probably used her old bloomers for dishrags."

Episode 49

Leaving Grand View: The Cardboard Box

My fondest memories center around growing up in Grand View, Idaho. But then, so do some things that should not happen to anyone, anywhere. Slavery shouldn't happen anywhere, but it did. Land should not have been stolen from the Indians (Native Americans), but it was. People should not be killed, but they are. We should be fair to everyone, but we're not. Bullying should not happen to anyone, but it does. The list goes on. Shit happens.

Did all these happen in Grand View, Idaho? Certainly not. And was Grand View unique from anywhere else at that time? Probably not. And was my experience different or worse than what other groups went through? No. I have no bull whip scars on my back. For a nation of immigrants, we are not tolerant to more recent arrivals. Are things worse now? I hope not. Some things are better; some things are the same, and some, God forbid, could be worse.

I write of experiences in my time (1935 to 1950) in Grand View. I make no apologies for what I say or if I'm not politically correct. If you should experience a little irritation with me, compare that discomfort to what I relate here.

"Hey, Black Bascos, why don't you go back where you came from?"

"Back into my mother's stomach?"

"Sheep lover! You fuck sheep!"

"Stop it. Shut your mouth."

"Garlic breath sheep fucker! Do you kiss your sheep?"

Fists flew. I'm not sure who won these scraps. Grand View won the verbal part because I reacted. I never told my mother the reason for the fights.

"What happened to you?" Mom would ask, "You and Frank been fighting again?" I'd leave it at that even though when Frank showed up, he had nary a scratch. At times like that, he knew. Sometimes these spiritual encounters would occur when two or three would taunt us and we both fought on the same side. Mom would say, "*Jesus, Maria, eta Jose!* It will be a miracle if both of you make it to be grown men." Frank caught my eye and for once we were on the same wavelength.

Some teachers were hired late in the year, sometimes late August, which meant they looked elsewhere first and as a last resort came to Grand View. Less schooled, they were probably rejected at the better schools. Of course, there were good teachers but most of those were gone the next year.

One teacher sent Basque students home or had them stay for detention if they smelled like garlic. Another didn't discriminate but made those caught chewing gum to draw a circle on the blackboard, place their wad of gum in the circle and then place their nose in the gum. They remained thus for several minutes.

Not only Basques, but Indians and Japanese as well had the good old welcome wagon hospitality visit them. First, the Indians, we stole their land and then we gave them a worthless piece back as a reservation to live on. We treated them as sub-human.

One Friday afternoon two high school boys and their girlfriends played hooky from school and went to a deserted farm in the desert above the irrigated farmland. The farm was abandoned when an earthquake, years earlier, dried up the artesian spring that supplied water to irrigate it. In the old dead cottonwood tree in the yard, they found a dead body hanging. As soon as the law determined that the male was an Indian, the investigation stopped even though circumstances indicated that Johnny Crow, an Indian, killed the younger buck, as males were called, because he had impregnated Johnny's daughter. Johnny was never questioned. If the body had been a white male, Johnny would have been arrested and tried. During WWII, Japanese-Americans were forced inland from U.S. coastal states (Hawaii, Alaska, Washington, Oregon, and California) to internment camps in remote places like Minidoka, Idaho, near Jerome. The U.S. government forcibly removed Japanese-American families from their homes and businesses, and then placed them in these camps because we were at war with Japan. Two high school Japanese boys, Sonji Kaga and Shozo Ano, enrolled in Grand View High School. The two were at school two days and no one talked to them. The third day, my brother, Louie invited them to join the other boys in a baseball game. The two gladly accepted and from that moment on in their eyes, Lou could do no wrong. Well into very old age, they kept in touch with Lou. Every visit, they said to Lou, "When no one talked to us, as if we had the plague, you were the first to speak to us and the only one to treat us as equals. You don't know how nice that moment felt." Goodbyes always involved big bear hugs and tears—from all three.

Half-way through my second grade, through sometime in the fifth grade, I was the only one in my grade level. In the fifth grade, Marilyn Walden joined the class, doubling its head count and becoming my first love, except she never knew it. Well, she knew it but I wasn't hers. Being a sheepherder, a Black Basco, was not the same as belonging to the Daughters of the American Revolution. Years later, she was my nurse in a hospital in Idaho. We chatted.

"Remember in school how you had the biggest crush on me?"

"Yeah."

"And I had nothing to do with you? Well . . . I was wrong. I'm sorry. I'm so sorry."

"Thank you." That made me feel so good, but I didn't tell her that I found better.

As I build my case against Grand View, my arguments may not be that convincing. But my final example involves bullying—and bullying to a degree way beyond torture. I gave some examples earlier with the fights over name-calling. Perhaps we all have experienced some aspect of it either as victims or as perpetrators, or maybe as both. But the bullying to the degree that my sister, Felipa, endured at Grand View should be against the law. All of us in the family were victims: Louie was, but his redeeming feature was his athletic ability, which helped the Grand View Devils (how appropriate!) win games. Frank and I were bullied, but the family moved and school life at Meridian High School was such an improvement. However, Felipa was so bullied and harassed, that she never was a happy person. She cried daily even though she was blessed with a wonderful daughter and three fantastic grandsons, all four with college degrees. The Grand View experience robbed her of a pivotal stage in development, which came to a head as she slipped into dementia. She wanted so much to be loved but had never learned how to cope with the hurt caused by bullying. I will never accept that the burden of her unhappiness was not due to evil that existed in Grand View, Idaho. I understand through a psychic medium that she is happy on the other side as she never was on this earth.

So, what was the point of this section? We were poor. Life was hard. Remarks hurt. But that is now gone. Was I also guilty of the same? I didn't taunt Hugh Hughes. But I did not include him in my dealings either.

As stated earlier, my fondest memories were my Grand View years. Thank you, Grand View. So what was the point of this story? Bad things happened to us that should not have. Bad things happened which are now good memories. Bad things have happened which are not the fault of anyone.

Grand View, you also gave me fond memories. I love you Grand View. The sight of Chatten Hill from our place and the road around the cemetery. And the Square Deal Store with gas pumps in front and the hotel above getting the first telephone and Mark Ryden's presence on the bench up town and people waiting for the mail to be distributed at the post office, or wondering if there really were whores upstairs in the Bank Club, and I ran out of fingers to list the memories.

Episode 50

Nemesio's Generosity

Part 1: A Sick Cow and Fay Bayfield

At times when Dad wasn't nearby, we overheard remarks about Dad made by others, be they Basque, or be they Red Hairs. Overall, they didn't upset us since most were favorable. So unless they were unkind, specified enough, or numerous enough, we forgot them.

One remark heard from the Red Hairs frequently was, "That God Damn Black Basco thinks we all want to work as hard as he does. If he does, he's got another thought coming: I'll do my share but not an atom more."

Another remark was, "You know, he is a cranky son of a gun, but you have to say he's a good worker."

"You are so right there! And his bark is actually misleading. Why, he is so friendly and easy to get along with. And you know—if someone needs help, he is the first there with help, and generous help at that."

Fay and his wife, Gertrude, and their sons, John and Bob, were our family's best non-Basque friends and yet there was a silent invisible wall. We never had them over for dinner nor they us, and yet, both did all sorts of favors for each other.

Frank (Jr) and I were at Byfields playing with John and Bob. In the course of the visit, I mentioned that a cow was down with milk fever—the fourth one now. The three that died were dragged to the pigs to eat. "One of our cows is dying with milk fever. They die once they get that."

Fay interrupted, "What did you say? Frank (Frank was the name the Red Hairs gave Nemesio. It was common practice to use American names) has a cow down with milk fever? Tell him to call the vet. Tell him ... No wait, I'll tell him. I'll tell him right now. Gertrude, I'm going over to Frank's for few minutes." He set out for our place on foot since the two homes were so close to each other.

He found Dad feeding the pigs. "Hello Frank, are you always busy?"

"Hello Fay," Dad answers, "What my kids do now?"

"No! Nothing. You have a cow down with milk fever? You know you don't have to lose the cow. Like I told you before; get the vet and he will give the cow an injection in the jugular vein. The cow will let out a bellow and run around the yard like a moose in heat. I'm telling you. Look, I'll pay the vet. If she does what I say, you pay for the vet. If she doesn't, I'll pay the vet and you aren't out one red cent."

"I'll tell you what. If that cow does what you say it will, I will pay the vet and you can have the cow and I'll throw in the bull calf too," Frank counter-offers.

"It's a deal, my stubborn Basco with one more item, the winner of this wager gets a ride in my wheelbarrow pushed by the loser from the loser's home to the winner's." Hands were shaken— the deal was made, Basco style.

Fay hurried home, got in his Model T Ford, and putted up the two miles to Grand View to catch the vet. Fay was lucky since it was a slow vet day and Dr. Wilson was about to close shop for the day.

"Damn tooting right, I wanna see the look on that Basco's face. In fact, I'll bring a gallon of 'rot-gut' these Basco drink. They call it *Vino Fino.*"

Doc put on his coveralls over his regular clothes and prepared the shot for the cow. He milked the small crowd for all he could. "Frank, where is this miserable creature, you call a cow? And Fay why do you wanna steel it? You know, this shot ain't gonna work. Where is the jugular vein? I'll stick it here."

The cow bellowed in her best "bellow" voice and sure enough did indeed run around, like a moose in heat, not that any of the three men knew what that was like. Suffice it to say that is not important, except to a bull moose.

"A miracle! A miracle." Dad got about as excited as a moose in heat. "Well, Fay, you now own one scrawny old cow, and one decent bull calf, and someone who will listen to you."

"No Frank. Just pay the vet and we're square—after I get my wheelbarrow ride, that is!"

"Fay. We shook hands on it. And you taught me something! Here, take a swig of Doc's *vino fino*." And off they went.

"Hey Boys. No charge from me. We need to do this more often."

"Agreed, except somebody else furnishes the cow next time."

The wheelbarrow ride with many a stop for *vino fino* was enjoyed by all three men plus Fay's family and Nemesio's family, with the sad subplot of Byfields plan to move.

Sad, indeed, was the farm auction and the last days of Fay and Gertrude and John and Bob. Dad bought as much of the Byfield farm machinery, hay, and miscellaneous items as he could, including their surviving horse, Babe. We had Jerry, the surviving member of our team, which gave us a complete team of Jerry and Babe.

And tears flowed as they left. The Byfields left to operate The Sunburst Hotel in Sunburst, Montana, fifteen miles from the Canadian Border. They stopped at our place with their homemade trailer pulled by their model T ford. As goodbyes were being said, Fay asked Dad to go with him where he had hidden the wheelbarrow, made Dad get in, and pushed him to our place. The old wheelbarrow, with Gertrude's ribbon attached, was given to Nemesio. The two men hugged and cried as did the two ladies and boys.

A few years later, Fay passed away and some years after that Gertrude remarried. She and her new husband paid us a visit. Even "Red Hairs" can be good people—damn good people.

Episode 50
Nemesio's Generosity
Part 2: Under New Management

In another discussion concerning Nemesio's traits, Basilio added, "And how about those two acres of fruit trees: mostly apricots and peaches—and that huge weedless garden—probably an acre in itself? The man may have been stubborn and cranky but you'll not find a harder worker or more generous man in America. Or Spain. Why, Nemesio would give you three or four bushels of fruit and ton of vegetables from his garden and refuse to accept a penny payment!"

"But you know, he probably should have charged something, since the family was so poor and with all those children. And the once-a-year-when-the-fruit-is-ripe friends took advantage of his generosity."

This would enter this pre-death eulogy from one person or another. At times, the contributor of this bit of wisdom may have been a little suspect in his own intentions.

Victorina, too, was not afraid of hard work and sacrifice, and would do anything for others. However, she did resent these annual visits from the freeloaders, especially from those visibly better off than her family. She decided that, except for people like close friends, children's teachers, the irrigation company ditch rider, and the like, there would be no more free handouts.

"But, I can't start charging now—people have come to expect it. It is like I've given them my word," Nemesio protested.

"But I can!" came her response. "You haven't given my word! And, neither have I!" As it happened, Nemesio was out in the field when the Browns came for some bell peppers. They picked a large box of the best peppers. As they were leaving, they asked the expected hollow question,

"How much do we owe?"

"Two dolla."

She was amused by the startled look on their faces as they scraped their pocket change for the money. It was obvious they had expected the usual, "Forget it. Nothing," which they had become accustomed to getting from Nemesio. Needless to say, Victorina was proud of her resolve and took credit for the absence of future Brown visits.

"Not only did they expect not to pay, they picked the biggest and best peppers, the ones I was allowing to redden and planned to can. Miss them? Are you crazy?" was her usual reaction to any mention of their absence.

As word got around that the Barayasarra produce was under new management, the quantity and frequency of these visits lessened. Some of the produce was taken in to the Square Deal Grocery and Department store and applied toward the family's monthly tab.

Episode 50

Nemesio's Generosity

Part 3: The Next Generation

Nemesio's generous character and the pride of not being cheap certainly rubbed off on his children. Continuation of Nemesio's practice, it was their usual practice to insist on paying the first round of drinks or to grab the group check at a meal, even though everyone may not buy a round of drinks, or even if some at the lunch may never have the opportunity to reciprocate.

"I'd rather pay more than my share," Lou would say, "than to be thought of as cheap!" While Lou was living in Seattle, working at Boeing Aircraft Company and I was in my freshman year at Seattle University, we often took long walks around the city—the longest being from the University of Washington area to the ballpark of the Seattle Rainiers. On one of these walks, near the waterfront with $3.00 between us to last three days until Lou's next payday, we encountered a beggar with one leg and the stump of the missing leg bandaged with what appeared to be blood oozing through the gauze bandage.

Without hesitation, Lou reached into his pocket and deposited the entire $3.00 into the coffee can on the sidewalk at the base of the beggar's foot. Not a word was exchanged between the two of us until we returned to their apartment.

"Now what?" Lou asked.

"I don't know!" I responded.

"You know what? He was a fraud: If there was fresh blood, he wouldn't be sitting in that dirt and not in a hospital."

"I wondered about that, too."

"Well. I'd rather be a sucker than to not give to someone in real need."

"Yeah, me too."

Well. The "now what" was three days of hunger and a good lesson in compassion. I wouldn't want to go through it again but I'm glad we did.

Episode 51
Field Biology Expedition
Part 1: Culture Shock

"We'll camp here," Dr. Robert Bratz, co-leader with Dr. Lyle Stanford, announced to the expedition. "The base of this gravel pit is about as flat a spot we are likely to find in this rain forest. Ladies' area to the right and men to the left." The first order of business at each campsite was the designation of ladies' and men's areas. At first we joked about it, at times it was ignored, but eventually, it was appreciated.

The caravan from the College of Idaho Field Biology Expedition, consisting of four cars with trailers, and two pickup trucks, one pulling a commissary trailer, carried twenty-four college students, two professors, and a graduate assistant. The group was on the sixth week of a nine-week plant identification expedition through Mexico.

By this time, the novelty of camping had worn off and the groups, with a couple of exceptions, had jelled into a living unit with individual students adhering to two major rules: (1) In Mexico, we were the foreigners, and (2) each was expected to do more than his/her share to make the expedition work.

The expedition was not all lectures, plants, collecting, and identification; we had the so-called tourist time, as well, although we did our best to separate ourselves from the typical American tourist—a pot-bellied, old man in Bermuda shorts, tacky Hawaiian shirt, sneakers, and six cameras around his neck. "*Norte Americano*" he was called by the polite Mexican, and "Gringo" by the rest. Souvenirs were a bargain with the exchange rate being twelve pesos to the dollar.

Although I had grown up in poverty, my experience did not match the poverty and misery I saw around me. Culture shock was generic to poverty shock.

"Don't give anything to anyone until we are ready to break camp." As cruel and cold as it seemed, this advice was carefully and religiously followed after the first time someone ignored it. In a desolate area, moments after someone gave a few centavos, we were setting up camp when we were suddenly surrounded by an unruly mob. Word quickly spread that some generous Gringos, somewhat loco in the *cabeza* were camped near the *camino*. Anything laid on the ground was considered a gift and would disappear. When two men began to take a tire off one of the cars, something had to be done.

"Don't show any panic. Act like we are setting up camp but do the reverse—take everything down and pack it up. We will drive off as if this is part of our usual routine. Watch the cars and tires. The crowd at this stage will not ignore you but it may become violent if we stay much longer."

As we drove away, we waved and some of the crowd waved back. I am sure this brush we had with a mob getting unruly and eventually violent reinforced some of the students' negative views. Someone asked Dr. Stanford where he learned how to deal with crowds. He said, "I don't know any more than you do. I was just as frightened as you. Frankly, I didn't think it would work. I gambled that if you all believed that I knew what I was doing, then maybe we could get away. And, by golly, we did."

Expeditioners learned how to cope with the reality of third world poverty in individual and varied ways:

"I don't give anything to anyone!"

"You can't help them all—there are too many!"

"I worked hard to get what I have. Why don't they get a job and do the same?"

"The Catholic Church is to blame: its policy on birth control is the cause—let the Pope take care of them."

"These people are so ignorant. They don't appreciate anything, anyway!"

"These people are so damn poor, why don't they have fewer kids?"

Etcetera! Etcetera! Each trying to rationalize and justify his/her own lack of compassion and sensitivity.

"These people don't want help: they have their pride."

PRIDE? Yes. There may be pride and dignity in the human spirit, but when an adult father stretches out his hand, "*Por favor?*" while his six- and ten-year-old sons are naked and must gather sticks to sell to help support the family and his daughter is crippled because there were no funds for corrective surgery, and he must beg for a few centavos from an eighteen-year-old *Norte Americano*, pride takes on a recessive role to the dominant need for survival!

The poverty, the diseases, the large hollow eyes of the children, naked, hungry, and working to help support the family made its mark on me. I knew poverty, but my poverty was luxury in comparison; my shack, a palace; my beans and potatoes, a gourmet feast; my suffering, ecstasy to what I saw around me. I could not get myself to buy the beautiful serape while walking past annoying, haunting pleas of "*Por favor, Señor.*" "*Madre de Dios, por favor.* "*Madre de Dios, ayuda a mi hijo.*"

As the caravan pulled into a petrol station, a skinny waif of a teenage girl, dress of repeat patches and tears, barefoot, carrying two naked babies, with those ever-present bulging bellies of malnutrition, walked up to the expeditioners. She and her babies had those goddamn hollow eyes. "No. I don't have any money!"

"No. Go away!"

"No. I'm sorry!"

"No. I'm all out of change right now!"

"No. I can't afford ..."

"No. Not today."

"No!"

"No!"

"No!"

As she neared me, I heard an inner voice cry out for her, "*Whatever you do for the least of my brethren, you do unto Me!*" I hoped she would go on by. I tried not to look at her and those babies, who would die anyway.

"God damn it, God! Why? Why?"

"*Por favor, señor?* My children, they are suffering. *Por favor,* could you not help? Maybe, you could take them with you to the Estados Unidos. They deserve a chance; they deserve better than this. Some medicine. Some food, *por favor.*"

Why did she single me out? I was down to my last fifty—probably the least anyone on this trip had. There she was before me—her eyes crying out, "*Here I am, the least of the least. Here I am, Jesus Christ to you. What are you going to do about it?*"

"I am so sorry, God, I can't . . . Here take it. It's all."

Turning, I bolted for the station's restroom; my eighteen-year-old pride would not allow that others should see me cry. I splashed cold water on my face and dried myself with my handkerchief. I returned to the caravan.

"You are so stupid."

"Man, are you stupid, or are you stupid?"

"You can't help them all."

"Don't come to me when you run short."

RUN SHORT? Run short? I gave her all I had. Run short?

"Hey, that was something you did—I couldn't have done it."

The caravan left the petrol station but pulled over in the next block since some nice serapes and souvenirs were seen. Everyone piled out—except me. I was drained of energy as well of cash. I sat there penniless, with the image of those sullen eyes forever burned in my brain. "I'm sorry, God, that I couldn't do more. Please take care of those kids."

Just then, the girl and her babies passed the car—on her way home with the equivalent of several months' pay. She was crying openly as she fingered a homemade rosary. She looked up at me, "*Gracias, señor.* You are indeed a Hand of God. You are Jesus! *Adios, amigo!*" She disappeared never to be seen again—but always to be remembered by me.

Episode 51
Field Biology Expedition
Part 2: Aztec Two Step

My college career started with a year at Seattle University, a Jesuit school, followed by a year in the Society of Mary Seminary. Finally, I transferred to the College of Idaho, a small Presbyterian College where I majored in Biology.

Every other summer the Biology Department had a Plant Identification Expedition through the Southwestern United States and Mexico. I attended the 1957 and 1959 expeditions. Besides learning the taxonomy of plants, we learned a great deal of geology, geography, history, and culture of a country, plus an excellent study of group dynamics among ourselves and with the majority population different from us.

I had a hard time with culture shock even as poor as I grew, it got to the point that I could not buy souvenirs and live with the haunting eyes of starvation I saw before me (part 1).

Let us get on to the Aztec Two Step account. Even at the young green age of twenty-two, I had the precursor to my later sleep problems. By the time we were in Mexico, District Federal (Mexico City), several students had the "Tourist's Disease," sometimes called "Montezuma's Revenge," or even "the Aztec Two Step." Whatever it was called, symptoms involved very serious diarrhea and serious dehydration—not good to have on a camping expedition in a hot country. Three of the students needed medication every two hours, day and night, administered by the designated student medics. However, the designated male medics could not wake up during the night. A substitute was needed to wake up and make sure the night "patient" took his pills.

"Let Jim do it, since he is awake half the night anyway." Bright idea, my sleep problems qualify me to dispense medications to those needing their fix during the night.

"I second the nomination."

"Sounds legal to me. Thank you, Jim."

"Does this count as my share of more than my share?"

"No. It still has to be more of your share of everything."

"I'll do it but it is really '*more than my share-squared*'. The jokes and humor are really getting bad."

Mike Nishitani was one poor soul under my care. I woke him and this prompted an upchucking urge on his part. He ran to the bathroom in his undies and I followed in mine. My mother always held my forehead when I threw up, so of course, I held Mike's forehead as he puked in the toilet. That alone looks questionable—two college kids in a stall together, making strange noises. Either Mike's mom held his head, or he was too sick to object. But when his partially digested evening cuisine began to exit through his oral cavity, my altruistic behavior tended to act in inverse correlation. I felt things coming up. Now I was, as they say in Joel, Idaho, "on the horns of a dilemma." Between the point of exit and the path of my projectile to the crapper, was Mike's head. What to do? I pulled the support of Mike's forehead and ran out of the bathroom to the balcony outside one of the windows. I don't know if Mike adjusted to the sudden loss of cranial support or not. I didn't care as I leaned over the wrought iron balcony and made appropriate noises—only the dry heaves. As my eyes dried, and I recovered, I, in my tighty whiteys, was overlooking an all-night sidewalk cafe across the street. No one on the expedition noticed except Mike, and he probably wasn't going to admit our midnight fling.

Episode 51
Field Biology Expedition
Part 3: Shark Attack

Dr. Lyle Stanford, co-leader of the expedition announced, "This is a good safe place to swim if you want. See that coral growing across the mouth of this inlet? Sharks will not cross since, through evolution, they have learned that if they brush up against living coral, the coral grows in their tissue as a parasite. By the way, it will grow in your tissue as well. If you walk on coral, wear your sneakers." We were camped at Guymas on the Sea of Cortez or as we on this side of the wall call it, Gulf of California. One unusual feature of the area was that desert vegetation existed right up to the water because of the Trade Winds blowing westward from land to sea.

On the west side of the inlet, a large cliff formation jutted out. Gary Goade, Mike Nishitani, and I walked up on the rock formation and sure enough, no sharks on the coral-protected side where we swam but on the other side we counted over a hundred. That is a lot of sharks. We continued walking up the coast in about a foot or two of water.

We came upon this three-foot long fish which was not afraid of us, and so we tried to catch it with our hands. It swam just enough to keep out of our reach. When it was swimming across the front of us, we saw it was a shark. We backed out into shallow water about a foot deep and were flipping it with our bath towels. It swam one way and then the other, and then, with no warning, headed right for us. Gary and I got out of the water, but Mike froze, lifting one leg up screaming, then the other, and screaming. The shark went right for him but, right at his legs, turned and swam away. Needless to say, Mike did come out at that moment. On the way back, he didn't get any closer to the water's edge than fifteen feet.

We teased him about it, "Was it your screams or did the shark get indigestion?"

"Hey, you monkeys took off and left me to fight him off, ALONE!"

Episode 51

Field Biology Expedition

Part 4: A Mule, a Skunk, and a Bat

The expedition was rich with experiences and it is not surprising that most of my college memories center around it. Let me inflict you with one more. Early in our journey, Dr. Robert Bratz announced, "a highlight for some of you will be a hike across the Grand Canyon from the South Rim to the North Rim which, incidentally, is a thousand feet higher than the South Rim."

"Some of us?"

"Yes. Some will be needed to drive the vehicles around through the Painted Desert and set up camp on the North Rim. We will be spelling out special rules you must agree to or you just don't go. For instance, we walk single file and no one passes the one in front. The slowest will be in front and we will walk at that person's pace. This will be the hardest rule for some of you to follow—we all have a certain pace and it is hard to walk at a slower pace. If we don't do that, it may cause the slowest to try to keep up and that could be tragic. Another point, if Dr. Stanford or I aren't convinced you are in shape, you won't go."

"How do we get in shape?"

"Good question. I was going to tell you next. You walk, any time you can. At lunch stops, grab your food and start walking; we will pick you up along the way. Eight weeks of walking and you will be in shape. You will hear more as we go along, especially during the geology lectures but, for now, the third rule is, don't piss any of us off."

And we did hear more—much more and a lot of geology, not only of the Grand Canyon, but of volcanoes, the Sierra Madre Occidental, Sierra Oriental, Sierra del Sur, and plate tectonics.

And we studied plants and we walked. We did all that except bathe a lot.

Anyway, we walked, we agreed, we didn't piss off anybody, we were selected, so we were dropped off at the South Rim, while Dr. Stanford and the others drove through the Painted Desert to set up camp at the North Rim in the Kaibab Forest. We left single file behind Sharon Messenger in the lead—she was the smallest and, therefore, probably the slowest. The 4:00 p.m. sun allowed us to do most of the walking in the shade. Plans were to camp at the bottom, hike in the morning until the sun was too direct, and then wait until the evening shadows to walk the rest of the way up and out.

On the way down, we passed our first mule train, the mules having the right of way. This meant we stepped to the outside of the trail and remained motionless as the mules passed, their bellies rubbing ours as they went by. We faced the trail, our backs to the sheer drop of a hundred or so feet. Standing on the outside of the trail allowed the mules to see us and not get startled. Whereas, next to the cliff, the mules may not see us as they round a bend until they were next to us and if startled, they may cause a problem. No one moved even when one mule shit on a hiker's foot.

We reached the bottom—well, sort of—we camped on the trail. Girls stopped while the boys walked past the next bend. This was to keep mating to a minimum.

Shortly after the sun decided to see what was happening with us, two of the girls came crashing through our area, screaming.

"There is a skunk eating our raisins! There's a skunk eating our raisins!"

A couple of brave, or stupid, boys went to rescue the girls and raisins from skunk attack, but immediately came back, not chased by hungry skunks but in laughter.

"There were no skunks—only chipmunks! But, but, the girls were throwing rocks at what they thought to be skunks," said one of the brave knights.

"If a skunk is eating the raisins, let him eat the raisins: Don't throw a rock at him," said the other.

"Now that we had our laugh for the day, granted a wee bit early, let's get going making use of the extra shade. We will actually reach the park-like area sooner than originally planned. We will hike out—and up in the afternoon shade. We will have breakfast and lunch at that time, a little short on raisins."

Holding it by the tips of its wings, someone brought a bat for the rest of us to examine. He put it down on a bolder and why I looked down at it with one leg on one side and the other on the other side, I sure as hell don't know. But I did just that.

"Be careful, bats are known to carry rabies and the fact that you found it during the day is not normal," Dr. Bratz warned us. I looked his way as he talked then back to the bat. The damn thing was gone. Then I felt it.

"Son of a bitch! Goddamn! Holy shit! Son of a bitch!" I prayed a litany of desperation. God answered in one of His mysterious ways—the bat fell out from the inside of my pant leg.

The bat had crawled up on the fabric of my Levis, away from my leg. At my knee, where jeans tend to be a tighter fit, I felt the goddamn monster, and although relieved it fell out so quickly, I could not rid my mind of thoughts—how far up my leg it may have gone, where it may have bit me, and where they would administer the rabies shots. And, of course, my discomfort was everyone else's moment of glee. God works in mysterious ways, alright. It was a move on His part to spare the girls further kidding about the raisins.

Episode 52

The Marriage of Jan and Boo

Family and friends of the bride and groom, from southern Idaho, gathered at St. Peter's Catholic Church of Shoshone, Idaho.

You might say Shoshone was a typical small town of the West. Yes, you might say that, but you would be wrong. Main Street was built around existing railroad tracks. Maybe nobody wanted the railroad to run through their part of town, so they built it far enough away and thus it was in nobody's back yard, and yet it ran smack dab through the middle of town. City slickers would stop on one side of the street to ask directions for a place located on the other side of the same street.

It was the first wedding that this groom ever attended and thus, it would be slightly redundant to say I was a bit confused about all the trappings of a wedding. Three daughters and three weddings later did little to alleviate that confusion. Each daughter rejected my, "Have you considered becoming a nun?"

Let me take you through the marriage of Jan Anchustegui and yours truly, Jim Barayasarra. Courtship's most lasting memory amounts to a blind date arranged by my friend, Gary Goade, and Jan's friend, Audrey Haga. It was to be a double date.

"How much cash do you have, Gary?" I asked the afternoon of the date. "Just what is in my pockets? I was going to hit you up. Why?"

We emptied pockets, and did the under-the-car seats and behind-the-cushions thing, and came up with a total of $2.81, hardly enough to rank us as the big spenders of 1961.

"Should we call it off? I can't see what else we can do," I said in my practical way.

"Wait a minute. I'll call up and say we will be running a little late. You know, too late to see all of the movie. We'll go through the drive-thru window and I'll order four small cokes while you keep the girls occupied with some dumb shit, which you're good at. And then we'll just drive around for the evening. Give me what you got."

A genuine stroke of genius on Gary's part. The boy handed Gary the cokes, and Gary returned the gesture with a fist-full of cash.

"Keep the change." And off we went before the girls could see the cashier counting out the coins, mostly pennies and nickels.

This extravagant first date must have done it. Jan and I were engaged a short time after that.

On May 27, 2018, we celebrated fifty-seven years of wedded bliss—and fights.

My bride was over thirty minutes late for the wedding and I received my first lesson of married life—wait, wait, and then wait—none of it for Godot.

Father Ricaldi, a Basque Catholic priest, did the honors and then we were off to the American Legion Hall after "seven wagons and a half" worth of pictures.

What else happened at that holy event? No water was changed to wine, although enough of the latter was consumed. And Felipa Uriona did fall down a flight of stairs. Perhaps not traditional memories of one's wedding, but nonetheless, memories of mine. I have always felt that after she traveled over a hundred miles to attend our wedding, we threw her down a flight of stairs.

And Jan's brother Alex and several other thug friends of ours insisted on packing our car for us.

"Janet, gimme your keys and we will load your car and have it at the door of the hall. That way you can visit with the guests a bit longer."

"Hey fellows, that will really help. I have to be in school in a few days." The keys were handed over and off they went, laughing and, in hindsight having too much glee.

"Good bye."

"Congratulations. Now, you two, we need a baby or two."

"Thanks for coming. Good bye."

"It was so nice of you to come."

"Wasn't Jimmy Jasauro wonderful? It was nice that you had a Basque priest."

"And Basque music. I love the accordion."

"Okay, folks, they have other matters to attend to." That was followed by more jokes and more laughter, elbow nudges and, "Ho. Ho. Ho." Part of their plan was to be back inside when we got to the car, although we did notice heads peering out the window to catch our reaction.

And reaction they did see. "What the holy shit did they do to the car?" The entire surface of that 1961 white Nash Rambler was covered with graffiti. That was Prank #1.

Prank #2 was evident when, four thirty-foot strands of what had to be every tin can in Shoshone clattered as we drove off. We were stopped by the local police on the next block, and made to take them off.

The officer wished us luck, followed by, "I could be giving you a ticket. And you can please remove your laundry from the trees on the next two blocks." We learned later the officer was alerted with the hopes he would issue a ticket. That was to be Prank #3.

Prank #4—Until the officer directed my attention to the laundry on the trees, I didn't notice it. Once noticed, that was all I could see: miles and miles of Jan's intimate under garments—many purchased for the occasion. Property owners came out to watch and provide a cheering section. "Suckers!"

After a quick stop at a coin car wash, we were officially on our honeymoon. We had planned to spend the night at Jordan Valley, Oregon. The six-unit motel was lucky to get two units a night rented.

"We need a room. How much will that be?" I asked.

"I'm sorry, we have nothing open."

"You are kidding! You can't be all filled up!"

"Well, we are."

"In Jordan Valley?"

"Yes, Sir. Every three years, the Dirt Bikers gather here for their fun-filled, hell-raising convention."

"And this is the weekend."

So, we left Jordan Valley to the bikers and drove west. "What does the map show in the way of towns coming up?"

"The only town on the map anywhere out here is Bend."

"Well, Bend, here we come. What does it show around Bend?"

"It looks like road bends."

Anyway Bend was gone in an instant. "What'll we do?"

"We can stop and spend the night in the gravel pit."

Jan started laughing: I joined her in one of those it-is-so-pathetic-all-you-can-do-is-laugh situations in a gravel pit where the road bends in Bend, Oregon.

Eventually, we progressed from joking about our day to nervous laughter to cathartic laughter, to more traditional amorous moves. Without detailing them, let it suffice to say, the disastrous day was to end quite the way most of it had gone. May 27, 1961 ended with this twenty-six-year-old virgin groom trying to comfort my twenty-three-year-old virgin bride. She in tears and me, my manhood in question.

"It's all right," I assured her, "there's more to all this than sex." While to himself, he thought, "Bullshit, is this what it is going to be?"

Happy to report, the next night in more comfortable surroundings, in San Francisco, dual virginity was indeed lost. The embarrassment and humiliating dual virginity that was at the time, later became a matter of highest personal pride.

After a couple of days in the San Francisco Bay area, we returned to our home in Lake Tahoe, Nevada, to finish out the school year. Two of my friends, Gary Goade and the high school coach, Gary Lundergreen, took extreme pleasure in waiting until we were home from school for ten minutes, and then came to visit, pounding on the door and loudly speaking to us.

"Open up. Love Birds."

"What's going on in there?"

"Do you need help?"

The only way to stop this litany was to wait at the door, ready to open it at the first knock or sound.

We decided to just let pregnancy occur on its own timetable. No birth control means were used. But month after month, nothing happened. An appointment was made with Reno's Catholic Charities office. And remember, we were that same couple that couldn't do the nasty out in a gravel pit near Bend, Oregon. Now we were checking into adoption. Mrs. Wang discussed the procedures and practices. She must have liked us—we passed her initial instinct test.

"Take these two forms to your doctors and have them fill them out. Mrs. Barayasarra, you go first to your doctor. If he finds nothing wrong with you, then you, Mr. Barayasarra, take yours to your doctor. We'll see you both when the forms are completed. It looks like you may be parents this coming summer. We try to match child and parent. Any questions?"

"What do the doctors do? What should we expect?"

"Nothing much, we just need a form filled out by the adopting parents—just a formality."

Basically, it states that you are unlikely to have children of your own. Mrs. Barayasarra, you need to see your doctor first. And then, if he doesn't find any reason that the female couldn't get pregnant, then you, Mr. Barayasarra, will go in to see your doctor."

What could that involve? A cough, a check of blood pressure, and maybe a finger up the ass—no problem. Was I in for a little surprise? Or what?

Jan went in for her appointment. I sat in the waiting lobby. The doctor walked her out, "There is no reason you can't produce as many babies as you want. You are in perfect health. The receptionist will fill out your form for you."

Then he turned to me, "Let's take a look at you. You may actually enjoy your exam," as he winks at me. "Let me listen to your lungs ..."

"Well, all I really need to look at is your sperm."

"Come on now! You have to be joking." What I really wanted to say was, "Listen, buddy, if you could have spent a night in a gravel pit where the road bends in Oregon, you would see that my sperm isn't likely to see daylight anywhere, let alone on a goddamn bathroom in a doctor's office with or without pictures of naked hos!"

"I-I – c-c-c-an't do ..." The words stopped and my mouth turned dry.

"Well, you can go home, use a rubber, do your thing, put the spent rubber in your armpit and bring it in."

"Am I in a bad dream? Does everyone who adopts have to do all this? Why? Why?"

"Adopt? You just want this form filled out so you can adopt? You didn't come in to see if you are sterile?"

"No, I don't care if I am sterile—in fact, if I have to jerk off in a bottle in your bathroom to find that out, it ain't gonna happen! Sure, I did that as a kid—but never, never, never, ever in a doctor's office."

He filled out the form, and off we went to see Amanda Ting, the caseworker we were assigned to at Catholic Charities. Two months later, we adopted a yellow thrift store blanket—with a baby inside. We gave back the yellow blanket to keep doing God's work. We kept the baby. Five months later, Jan was expecting—have you ever heard of that happening?

Episode 53
Three Tahoe Teachers Returning in a Blinding Snowstorm: All See Somethin'

It was very late Sunday evening and classes started the next morning after Christmas break. There were a few snowflakes in Boise, Idaho, but the snow had been increasing steadily and it was sticking around Winnemucca, Nevada. My brother Lou purchased a Corvair and although nervous as the snow piled up, he was pleased how it drove in the snow. We turned right at Winnemucca to the main highway west to Reno, where we would turn south to Carson City, and then over the Sierra mountains to Lake Tahoe. There was no question now that the weather was nasty and would get worse. Traffic had dwindled down to an occasional car, probably someone as desperate as three Tahoe teachers.

"Don't you think we should get a motel and drive tomorrow during the day?" Jan suggested.

"Three teachers would be out and they have a problem if one is out," Lou answered. Jan remained quiet even though each time we passed a motel, she made the same request with a little more urgency. Lou answered saying the same thing.

And I think I asked the same thing over and over. One of those questions a person often asks but doesn't really care is, "How does the car handle?" And they receive the same answer each time, "Great."

We would all go silent and remain silent as we looked out the windshield at the snowstorm. It was relentless, showing no mercy. The moon was in new moon phase and the light from our car and other occasional cars on the road created a surreal eeriness. If it weren't so pathetic for the three of us, it was beautiful. I don't think any of us noticed, or if we did, we kept it to ourselves. During those quiet times, I wasn't the only one impressed by the situation: we experienced the storm completely.

"WHAT WAS THAT? Don't stop!" Lou swerved to miss it, slid off the road, fish tailed, and came right back on the road

"Just a hitchhiker," Lou says.

"That was no hitchhiker," I say. Jan agrees.

"It was a hitchhiker."

"If that were a hitchhiker, you would have hit something—you drove right through it."

"A ghost," Jan offers.

"I agree. A ghost."

"That wasn't a ghost. When have you seen a ghost?"

"Right now," we both answered.

"It was a hitchhiker, period."

We each described it—we saw the same thing—a human-like, spirit-like grotesque, long armed thing. I learned something about Lou. Even if his senses saw something, he is not going to admit it. I, too, would accept a natural explanation first if it fit. It didn't here, so here I agreed with Jan. IT WAS A GHOST.

UNTIL—until someone mentioned methane gas coming out of the ground in that area. Years earlier I saw ghostlike gas emissions in that area. I then remembered stories of the will-o'-the wisp.

What did we see? A demon, a ghost, or a hitchhiker. Two of us agreed it was not a hitchhiker and we agreed it was a ghost at the time. However, I had forgotten stories of the will-o'the-wisp until someone mentioned them. I remembered seeing methane gas coming out of the ground in that area. A natural explanation Well, we have hitchhiker, ghost, or a will-o'-the wisp— one vote for each.

Episode 54
A Wee Bit of Genetics

Nemesio had a big nose and I needed no DNA test—I was his: passed the Rudolph Red Nose test with one look. My second daughter, Lisa, kept the trait going. And she started a father/daughter "YOU HAVE A BIG NOSE" kidding game between us.

I found this ugly Santa Christmas ornament: It was indeed ugly with this great big nose—I hope I didn't spend over a dime for it. She put it on the tree every year. Once I knew she did, I looked for it every Christmas.

Several years later she found these plaster of Paris, one-foot-high, giant nose bookends. She handed them to me at the airport as we were catching a flight home. I had to include them with my carry-ons. As I was checking in, a security gentleman with plastic gloves followed me carrying one of the noses, "Sir! Sir! What is this?" His face white as the plaster, his voice trembling.

"A nose," I answered, not trying to be smart ass.

"Please come with me," his trembling body said. He led me to a room with very thick walls, away from the crowd. They suspected a bomb. I was frisked again and the nose was thoroughly examined and finally, I was allowed to proceed with my noses. He had to escort me away from the customers so that if it were a bomb, only the two of us would die. Wasn't it nice he was so afraid that I might get blown up?

We inherit many traits. Another trait—at least I think it as a trait—runs in my family. I call it "being a counter." My brother Lou would count cars going past his place as he sat in his yard. Sometimes he would keep track of more than one category. I do it also, I count steps in a stairway, even when I know how many from before. Lisa with the nose does it also. So does her son, Zachary. One day as I was teaching class, my cell phone rings, "Excuse me class, Hello."

"Dad, this is Lisa. I know you're in class but I'm at the dentist's. There are 3,284 pocks in the ceiling tile."

"Thank you. I love you. Good bye." Then to the class, "There are 3,284 pocks in the ceiling tile at the dentist office. How is mitosis different from meiosis?" You know what—that interruption was so absurd that everyone remembered all about mitosis and meiosis since they remembered that we discussed it with the interruption.

I include the following incident, not that it has anything to do with anything, but only because Lisa's call during class reminded me of it. I taught a botany class for a class of eight students, two were foreign. I repeated the class for the two students and anyone else who wanted the extra help. Uthen from Thailand and Sumeko from Japan were my foreigners.

Uthen had a question, "The statement that viruses can be used to control pests. What are pests? Is that like pets?"

"Ah! Ha!" I thought. "Easy confusion for a foreigner. Like Mom and Mother is fat!" I thought I understood his problem. I wrote pets and pests on the black board and started to point out the difference.

"Is that like, American expression, piss on you?" This came from Sumeko in her perfect Japanese accent.

I added piss on the board and defined all three words. We all enjoyed class that day. Lest you think I wasted class that day, we well made up for the time in extra sessions. On the next exam, they all had no problem with remembering the botany lesson of the day as they all associated it with "pets, pests, and piss."

Episode 55

Irrigating with Jesus

After our marriage, May 27, 1961, and I finished course work for a master's degree from the College of Idaho, we were to spend the rest of the summer in a log cabin at the Anchustegui summer sheep ranch (between Fourth of July and Fischer Creek north of Sun Valley and south of Stanley, Idaho, in the beautiful Sawtooth Mountains). I was promised a very uneventful time: a chance to ride horses, attend the Stanley Saturday Night shit-kicking dances, time to relax and to take in the breathtaking beauty of the area, as well as the new bride.

Well, I was hoodwinked: although the area was as beautiful as described, the Stanley dances were indeed shit-kickers. I rode horses with no owner's manuals. It was not the least bit uneventful, and it was not a place to relax.

Let me give you an example of the mentality of the local all-year residents. There's Mable Louise Cutter, a lady who had tired of her husband; so much so, she ran him off her place by shooting the dirt at his heels with the good advice, "don't you dare darken my place again, you miserable, shit-eating, foul-mouthed, cocksucker! If you ever do, I swear to aim a little higher and raise your voice a notch or two."

"I'm going! I'm going! Don't be so—so negative all the time!"

Then, at a local bar, where the account was told nightly, Spot McKensey, with his usual onedrink-too-many moments, announced that all Old Lady Cutter needed was a good stiff one, "why, hell oh mighty, I might just have what that old gal needs, and I'm going right up there to get a little poontang." Nobody thought he was in any shape to find or to reach her place, let alone make any such offer to her. But he did.

"Hey, Mable Louise, how you getting along, up here all alone?"

"Just fine, Spot. Why you so concerned about me after all the years we've known each other?"

"Well, Mable Louise, it has been a month since Ezra left these parts and you, er—well, you ain't got none for quite a spell now, and I come up to see if I could be of some help, if you know what I mean."

"No, I ain't interested, Spot. So you just turn your miserable flea-bitten self around and I will make out like you dint say nothing. If you know what I mean."

"Ah, come on Honey Pot," as he moves over to her and puts his arms around her from behind, and tries to kiss her, "I'm all ready fir ya!"

"Will, I ain't ready fir you, you pathetic jug of skunk piss! Not now, never wuz, and never will be. Git your goddamn hands off me!" as she elbows him in the gut, turns around, and knees him in the balls.

"Aw, come on Baby, why you got to be that way?" He follows her to the woodshed as if this is all part of the ritual of getting a piece of ass.

She retrieved a rope, lassoed him, dragged him to the tree, and tied him to it. It was not much of a struggle for her since she was a strong as a mama grizzly bear, he had too much to drink, and he still thought it was part of her playing hard-to-get. She then jumped in her pickup and left for Boise for a week to see her sister.

The next day at the bar, the conversation was again about Mable Louise, and someone asked, "Didn't old Spot go up there to take care of her needs?" Laughter breaks out and someone else buys a round of drinks.

"Wait a minute. Seriously, have any of you seen Spot since then? He wasn't in the best condition, you—may have rolled his pickup into the Salmon River or something. If someone will keep me company, I'll drive up there to check."

The two men left for the twenty-minute drive to Mable Louise's place. "You know, Spot had to be one dumb shit to go up there all liquored up like he was."

"Almost there—well, at least he didn't run off the road. There's her place. I can see that big old willow in her yard."

"What the hell is—something is tied to it—it's a person. Holy Shit! It's Spot!"

It was indeed Spot McKensey, barely alive, barely conscious, slumped down. One man runs to the house for water as the other cuts him loose.

"There's no one there," he yells as he runs with a pot of drinking water for Spot, "Looks like she's been gone for some time."

"Goddamn Bitch! How can anyone be so cold?" The driver answers, "Tie a goddamn human to a tree and leave. Go back, use her phone and call the sheriff. Get some blankets for Spot to lie on in the back of the pickup. Tell him to meet us on way to Mable's place. I hope we're not too late. Goddamn it Spot, why couldn't you keep your pecker in your pants? Oh God! Please help us."

Spot survived, he did. The doctors at Sun Valley said it was a miracle that he did, especially as drunk as he was to start. Mable was not charged, since Spot was too embarrassed to press charges. That was typical of the year-round locals.

* * *

Jesus, one of the Anchustegui Basque employees, was the irrigator of the Fischer Creek meadow, which only became a problem in late summer when water became scarce. A plank diversionary dam was used to divert water to the Anchustegui property.

Jesus was getting ready to go change the water set one evening, when he invited me along with him to keep him company. We could try to visit in Euskara since he spoke minimal English, and I butchered minimal Euskara. I accepted the offer since Jesus was interesting, and if I stayed at the cabin, I was sure Jan would find me some cleaning to do.

He drove the jeep to the first set.

"*Mekowen Dios!*" (Spanish swear word which, loosely translated, means "Oh! That was not nice"). There was a trickle of water flowing which meant the Taylors, upstream, pulled out one of the planks in a diversionary dam, which resulted in less water to the Anchustegui meadow and more to theirs. "We'll have to ride up there and replace the plank, if we are to get any water," he tells me as we get into the jeep.

We arrived at the dam a few minutes later and, sure enough, a plank had been removed. Jesus replaced it and we headed for the jeep when, just as in the shoot-'em-up western movies, three sons and their boss lady mother rode down from the hills and surrounded the jeep, two with hangman nooses, and all four with holstered pistols. Jesus grabbed his irrigation shovel and was about to strike the boss lady off her horse.

"Don't!" I yelled at him. "You do that, and if we aren't killed on the spot, you will be in trouble with the law. Right now, it is Eusebio's problem: you don't want to make it yours, too. Let the lawyers decide."

"What can we do then?"

"Just get in the jeep and start to drive back to the cabin." He threw the shovel in and started the jeep, put it in gear, and we moved toward the horses in our way. Three of them, the ones with the men, backed out of the way, but Boss Lady, with a litany of the most colorful swearing this side of Hell, tried to get her steed to chest bump the jeep. The steed had more sense than Miss Sweet Lips and he, too, backed away. We drove away and were surprised that no bullets were fired after us, only her parting words, "Get the fuck out of here, you two garlic eatin', pee smellin', illegal shipjumping, pimple-prick sheep fuckers!"

Jesus never asked me to go with him after that. Eusebio probably forbade him to do so or maybe he had another job for me. Did I say another job for me? It was two weeks until shippen—Basque pronunciation of shipping—when the fatted lambs are separated from their mothers and shipped to Omaha or Ogden, and the ewes are divided into three groups: (1) those healthy enough for another year in the mountains; (2) those healthy enough to be sold to farmers with ewes to be kept on farms; and (3) those barren or not strong enough even to be farm raised. This last group was sold, as the herders put it, "to Campbell Soups to be used in chicken noodle soup." One elderly Basque, employed by Eusebio, herded a band of two thousand ewes plus that many or more lambs near the cabin and corrals. Rather than stay with the sheep, each night the sheep were corralled and each morning, the old gentleman showed up and took the band out to graze. However, the old man fell and broke his hip and leg.

What to do? To hire someone for two weeks would be difficult, if not impossible. Eusebio looked at his son-in-law; a Basque and son of a herder with a great reputation as a herder; a healthy male doing nothing but eating his food; and there he was, the dumb shit.

"Hey, Jim. You are going to be a sheepherder—for two weeks until shippen'. There's not much to it: the ewes automatically know where to go. You will use Domingo's horse and dog and leave here about six in the morning and return six at night. The horse is Chalie and the dog is Txo Txo. You start in the morning."

I was up, breakfasted, and about to saddle Chalie. I put the blanket on the horse's back and threw the saddle on and began to tighten the straps. "There, that should do it." I put a foot in the stirrup, grabbed the saddle horn, and swung my other leg to get on. The next moment, I was on the ground under Chalie with the saddle on the horse's belly. Rather than worry about getting kicked by the startled horse, I was more concerned that someone saw my folly. Jan came out to see me off and she saddled the horse for me.

Chalie, Txo Txo, two thousand plus sheep, and a brand new sheepherder set out for day one on the range. Can you imagine how far a couple thousand sheep can spread? There were sheep as far as I could see. "That's not good," I thought to myself, "so, what to do?" The horse, dog, and neophyte herder rode around the band, driving the sheep toward the center. I'm sure, if truth be known, the sheep gained more weight in the corral with no food than they did with this herder. The long two weeks finally, and mercifully, came to an end. And, at the age of twenty-six, I, Doctor-to be, retired from the sheepherding business, at that moment.

If Jesus calls you to go irrigating with Him, you must answer the call.

Episode 56

A Young Man, a Sexy Lady, a Mom, and a Nun

Josefina was a very sexy, sexy, sexy lady and which nobody would deny. Many a double-take marked the neophyte male to the dances. Those who knew of her, while able to control the double-take, could be cited with a somewhat longer response of eye muscles. Of course, she was aware of her charms. She put on her well-rehearsed spontaneous show many times during the evening.

To one of these Basque dances, my mother, my sister, my brother Mike, and I went. We were sitting at the edge. She came over and to Mike, who was standing by, now says, "These young heifers, with their nice titties have nothing on me. I can compete with any of them—and I would win every time, what do you say to that?"

"Let me see them!" Out she plops one.

"Mi-ke!" Mom interrupts as she makes Mike a two-syllable word.

"Don't worry Mom, someone has to put these young studs in their place!" as she moves on to her next show.

At another place where we lived, we had another lady who, with the help of silicone, had greatly augmented things. My kids attended St. Mary of the Angels Catholic School. She must have been a Catholic since she was working the blanket raffle at the school's Octoberfest. She wore a crochet mine skirt and top. I wondered which would win, silicone or yarn. I moved on and met two young nuns, who taught my kids.

"Oh, Sisters, what order of nuns wear pink habits?" I asked them.

"Pink habits? I never heard of any. Are you sure they weren't street clothes, you know we are allowed to wear regular clothes these days?"

"Oh no, Sisters, these weren't regular street clothes. They were special uniforms."

"Pink habit. We'll check it out and let you know."

"Thank you, Sisters." And off they went to check. And off we went on our way. I pictured Sr. Ann and Sr. Mark Ann reaching the blanket raffle booth. Says one, "I don't see any nuns here at all, do you?"

"No," says the other. "No nuns here. The only person in pink is—oh, no! Do you suppose that's the nun in special uniform?"

"I give him credit, for having. . ."

"Ah be careful; we are nuns!"

"The nerve, you didn't let me finish. Let's get him for that."

I was about to get on one of the rides and here come two nuns yelling, "Mr. Barayasarra, you're awful." Each grabbed an arm and shook the dickens out of me. I would say shake the hell out of me but they are nuns. You know what, I bet they enjoyed it.

Episode 57
There Will Be No Shenanigans
with Barayasarra and Hannigan

I ran for political office once, I won once, but before I could celebrate my victory, I was charged with nepotism and I resigned in disgrace as a newly elected member of the Olean Public School Board. Other than the fact that I ran as a team with Helen Hannigan, with the catchy sound bite as the title for this episode, there is nothing to say. End of story.

Oh all right, I will fill you in on the sordid, sleazy details of my own Tammany Hall—after all, who can I embarrass now? My brother—who was so concerned that I may just embarrass the family—is gone now. Do you suppose he had a legitimate cause for concern?

During my tenure as a student working on a doctorate in biology, my wife was the sole support of our family with her teaching income. As if that weren't enough to keep her off the street, we took in Latif Chafik, an eight-year-old boy from Morocco, to raise as the son we never had. Latif, not being a citizen of the United States, did not come with foster care stipend. Technically, he was in this country on a student visa. Just one more mouth to feed.

Olean hired a new superintendent of schools, Dr. Oscar Pultz, who ruled by wining and dining the "important" people of the district, then quietly getting his new friends to run for the Board, replacing those he didn't agree with. Once he had a majority on the Board, he went after controlling the teachers—what better way than by fear? He singled out thirty-five teachers to fire, by not renewing their contracts. The thirty-five were notified by letter the last day of school prior to the two-week Spring Break, giving them the option to resign by the first day school resumed. Jan was one of the ones chosen. What better person to pick—new to the state from Idaho and therefore with little roots or reason to fight back. Most of the others were also from out-of-state and had similar vulnerabilities about them. The tactic worked with those not released, as no one wants to rock any boat which still carries them.

Little did he know that a graduate biology student was not to be easily intimidated, although we later learned that some pressure was hinted that the university was to drop me from the graduate program.

By God, if my dad were not going to cower to bullets and my mother to a poisoned cake, Mr. Pultz sure as hell is not going to find that I learned the trick of rolling over easily. Friday before the Monday deadline, the teacher's union, few of whom wanted to rock the boat they were on, found out they were scheduled to be on the next boat to be torpedoed. Word was sent to the few who had not resigned, not to do so—that a petition was to be circulated asking for HIS resignation. This not only made the local paper (wined and dined editors, et al.) but both this and the paper from Oscar's previous appointment were very similar, meaning they were used quite successfully over the years. A group of ex-teachers came down to help with the petition drive. Door to door recruits were used to canvas the area for signatures—myself included. I am happy to relate that I collected by far the most signatures—my research of the liverwort bulb production being put on hold.

For a very brief period, I served subpoenas on several of the Oscar cronies, until my cover was blown away with my high petition visibility. Even then, it was amusing to see grown men duck out one door as I entered another. Is politics dirty? "You betcha boots, *y zapatos también*."

When the shit began to pile up around the Pultz outhouse, an open "town hall" type of meeting was scheduled. The school auditorium was packed with Pultz and his gang sitting at the upstage side of a clothed table from one end of the proscenium arch to the other. On the surface, it was Christ and the Last Supper. In reality, Judas sat in the center with this board member leaning this way and that one leaning that way. Don't these people see that sort of thing, or is it deliberate on their part? I got quite a laugh when I pointed it out.

Father Duncan, an Episcopalian priest and one of the well-dined and wined, came over to me at another meeting to explain the facts of life to me. "How are you, Jimmy?" he started, "just what is your problem with Dr. Pultz? He's trying to improve schools."

"And firing my wife is the way to do that?" I asked. "Father, you are so goddamn full of shit, you genuflect when he comes in the room."

"You are going to say that once too often, Jimmy," taking a step closer to me so that we were literally chest to chest, or belly to belly, actually. "You are going to say that once too often."   "Go ahead, hit me, Dunkie," I threw in, hoping and afraid he may do it.

Fast forward . . . Helen Hannigan and I ran as a team against Mike Vanniny and Elizabeth Prettyman, also running as a team. Election night results were as follows:

Hannigan – 1,799, Barayasarra – 1,399, Prettyman – 789, and Vanniny – 492

And talk about political power! Strange as it seems, Mr. Pultz, excuse me, Dr. Pultz, offered Jan her job back, pending School Board approval. We did nothing to have them reconsider, except with an election. Do we party now and join the team? Not so fast. "It ain't over, 'til it's over." Thanks, Yogi.

Well, it wasn't over. In Olean, if a Board member's spouse is to be hired, a vote of six, instead of the usual majority of five, was needed. And of course, I ran only to get Jan's job back—or that is what it was made to look like. The job offer was made to Jan, while a news item was sent to the paper in the same mail as the nepotism charge. Clever how we were again screwed, making it look like we outsmarted ourselves.

And Father Dunkie told me, "Resign and Mrs. Barayasarra will only need five votes then. I will vote in favor—thus giving you five votes."

Our lawyer friend advised, "You have no choice. You have been outsmarted. Resign and let their vote go where it will. One positive note, Jan will not be bothered again. However, your one accomplishment, of having the superintendent's office relocated to the old unused restroom in the basement, may be changed back as well."

"And that's all folks!" to quote either Yogi Berra or Bugs Bunny. I swear now and then that the only shenanigan was the relocation of Oscar's office. Dr. Pultz and his business manager resigned within a year and he died in his Virginia home.

Episode 58

Somewhere, Out There is my Son

Somewhere my son exists, an unusual lad in that he has a wonderful story to co-write with me—if I live long enough. If not, he must go it alone. Where is this land of enchantment which ushered him forth to my family and joined us with God's love? And who is he, pray tell?

Why was he not adopted? Lord knows we tried. It was a complicated story and varied forces of blood and politics of two nations were involved. He came on a tourist visa and left in New York City with an uncle who was to take care of his Islam training while a home would be found for him nearby. His visa had to be changed from tourist to student to take care of immediate legal status. So that took care of legality as long as he was a student—from the age of eight to his twenties. Ironic as it may appear, as many problems exist with keeping track of immigration, our government can keep track of one individual.

Abdellatif Chafik is his name. Morocco is the land of enchantment. He was placed in several homes prior to ours. Some, including ours, thought he was for adoption. For one reason or another, they did not work out. One of the most unusual situations was a very wealthy home which Latif said treated him as a pet rather than as a son.

Now, how unlikely would we be as a choice for an adoption or placement family even though we adopted our first child and were scheduled to receive a black or biracial child? (Maybe I answered my own question.) Anyway, here are the reasons that I think would rule us out. Jan was the sole supporter of a family with two adults and three daughters. Latif could not be placed as a foster child since he was not a citizen. This meant one more person to feed and clothe on already stretched funds. I was a graduate student working toward a doctorate in biology and unemployed.

Second, he was Moroccan and Muslim—and we were Basque and Catholic.

I knew very little about his faith and his culture. Monsignor Kaiser, the priest who arranged a scholarship at St. Bonaventure for Latif's uncle told us, "Don't try to convert him. His uncle is responsible for his faith."

He spoke only Arabic and French—no English. I thought he was extremely shy. My wife worked with him, along with his teacher, and had him not only caught up to grade level but at the top of his grade.

As I said, we were not the first to audition for the role of his family. He loved Monsignor and wanted to have him as a father. Monsignor was about to give in. "You have exhausted all potential homes?" he asked Frank..

"That's right, Monsignor."

"Well, maybe it's to be! You're sure?"

"All I can come up with, is this family who have kids in my kid's class."

"He doesn't have two pennies to rub together."

"Why is he still a maybe? Let's have the rest of the story."

"His oldest daughter is adopted. He was scheduled to adopt a black boy, before he went back to school. Now that's postponed. Next week is Thanksgiving break, he needs to be checked out."

"How about, this evening, Thursday? They can take him to McDonald's, spend the evening with him, get him back home by bedtime. Then, pick him up after school tomorrow for the weekend, back home, Sunday bedtime. Again Wednesday for the break. If that works, we have a home." Monsignor rattled off as if he had a script. The conspiracy was planned.

They were at our place before we got home. Frank spoke, "Monsignor, this is the Barayasarras. Jan this is Monsignor Kaiser and this handsome gentleman is Latif Chafik. May we come in?" Once inside and seated, Latif took his coat and folded it neatly it and placed it beside him on the couch. "Monsignor would like to speak to you. Is this a good time?"

"Yes," I answered trying to hide the "what choice do I have."

"Latif, this lady is Mrs. Barayasarra and this is Latif."

"Hi. Welcome, Latif. What a handsome boy you are," as she hugged and kissed his forehead. I was next. "And these are his daughters, Christina, Lisa, and Mary."

Mary grabbed his hand and all three took him to play with their toys. Years later, he told us that he liked us right then. "First," he said, "The lady hugs and kisses me, the only time a grown lady ever did that. And then the girls take me to their toys and let me play."

"And what about me?"

"Oh you were the man who had one big eye and one little eye." I looked in the mirror and sure enough, I did.

Back to the plan: He was left with us. We went to McDonalds and I ordered hamburgers and near bedtime, we took him home. "See you tomorrow." We picked him up right after school and had him all weekend and on Sunday made sure he was home at his bedtime. Now the plan was we pick him up Wednesday before Thanksgiving and if everything worked at that time, he would move in with us.

Sunday we took him back. That night, he ran away and was wandering around. An old gentleman picked him up. Frank gave him a card with his name. Latif gave the card to the driver who knew Frank, so he drove Latif there.

Monday, when I came home from St. Bonaventure University, there was the caseworker's car waiting with an eight-year-old Moroccan lad and his belongings. Now, you tell me, just because my wife didn't give birth to him or because he wasn't adopted that he is not my son. I will glare at you through my lopsided eyes.

Episode 59
Dietrich, Take Off Your Shoes

When a couple of Idaho potatoes decided he should accept the assistantship offer from St. Bonaventure University in western New York State to work toward a doctorate in biology, and she would get a teaching job to support this endeavor and their three small daughters, neither knew how close to the local yokel stereotype they would become—and how long this opening sentence would be. They soon learned that they too had stereotypes of people in the East, especially New York people, who are mugged, robbed, and shot on a daily basis. Being the ones moving from discrimination to acceptance in the West did not give them the opportunity to look down on anyone else. The adoption agency from Spokane, Washington, had scheduled us to adopt a black, male baby. Had we and they followed through, I often wondered if the poor child would have survived our ignorance, although I end up regretting that we didn't do it.

Anyway, I accepted the assistantship and Jan landed a job teaching fourth grade for the Olean, New York schools. In her class of thirty students, she had one black male, Dietrich Gilbert, whose mother had several babies, each with a first name beginning with "D," all raised by a saintly grandmother who did the best she could.

Jan immediately took a liking to Dietrich who, to most teachers, was a troublemaker and not worth their time. Each night she came home with stories of what mischief Dietrich did that day and felt bad the days she sent him to the principal for discipline. Most of the time, she had a hard time scolding him; he would either use the beaten puppy look on her, or would make the funniest remark, often denoting wisdom far beyond his behavior.

He walked to school, wearing overshoes or boots. But, unlike the other kids, he kept them on all day. Not knowing why, Jan said nothing about the boots day after day, even though many times a week, she stopped to offer him a ride to school. Once spring started, she would suggest:

"Dietrich, you would be more comfortable if you would remove your boots inside the building," and each day he would agree but would keep his boots on.

"Dietrich, it is mid-March and I don't think you will need to wear your boots anymore this year." And, again, the advice was ignored.

"Dietrich, please take your boots off inside. You will be more comfortable."

"Mrs. Barayasarra, you ask me to take my boots off each day and the reason I don't is that I don't have a pair of shoes—the boots are all that I have."

"Oh, I didn't know." All through the day, that's all she could think of, "the kid had no shoes!"

I stopped by at the end of the day to pick Jan up, since that day I had the car. Dietrich stayed after school as he often did to pound the chalk out of her erasers, not through detention but rather to show Jan he liked her. She called me out into the hall and told me about the shoes or lack thereof: "Can you take him down to Lester's and get him a couple pairs of shoes?"

"Come Dietrich, I have a surprise for you ... Jump in the car." He looked puzzled as he did not know me as well as he knew Jan, but he did as he was told. "All right, we are getting you some shoes." We went into Lester's Shoe Store and to the salesman, "this young man needs a couple pairs of shoes—sneakers, whatever."

"How do these look to you? This is our most popular brand among kids your age."

"I like these a lot—I can step up in those." That was easy.

"Do you have church shoes, young man?" I asked.

"You gonna get me two pair of shoes?"

"I sure am!" And I did.

"You took the kid without permission? You could get in a whole lot of trouble, kidnapping, abduction, molestation ..." That seemed to be the thought on everyone's mind.

"How can buying a kid a couple pairs of shoes be—be molestation?"

"Doesn't have to be—just somebody say it was—anyway, it was stupid of you!"

"My Grandmother wants to speak to Mr. Barayasarra. Can he stop by at our place tomorrow after school?"

"Oh, my God! Did she take it wrong? I wonder what she wants." I worried all day. After an eternity, "tomorrow after school" finally arrived and I stopped by at the Gilbert residence.

"Hello, Mrs. Gilbert. I am Jim Barayasarra, Mrs. Barayasarra, Dietrich's teacher's husband. If I offended you by buying the shoes, I'm sorry. That was not my intention."

"Oh, no, Mr. Barayasarra. That was a wonderful thing you did for our Dietrich. Mrs. Barayasarra is his favorite teacher ever and you both are so kind to him. You did something good for us so we want to do something good for you."

"It's not necessary, Mrs. Gilbert. I was happy to be of some use."

"Hush! Our church, Shiloh Baptist Church, is having a special service this Sunday with a dinner in the basement afterwards. I am making chitterlings and you and your family are invited to attend. That is the only way I can show my appreciation so we will see you Sunday at the 11:00 service."

What to do? What to do? I was such a brat to my own mother and would not eat much of the ethnic foods prepared—tripe, brains, pig's feet, fava beans, blood sausage, and, worst of all, mountain oysters, which are lamb nuts cooked in scrambled eggs. That dish looked like big grey snot in yellow eggs—ugh! Now here I was facing pig guts—what to do?

Behavior I had as a child just was not acceptable in an adult. Finally, I psyched myself up with the following determination: I will eat the damn things and I will act as though I enjoy them. After all, others will be eating them and liking them. They will in no way be harmful. I made it through a plateful and was quite proud of myself when Mrs. Gilbert took my plate and brought a plate full of pig guts. I learned something about black women, never give them your plate for seconds—they don't know what a serving is and will give you enough to keep half the population of Africa alive or enough to put a poor Hispanic person on his death bed. I survived.

Dietrich even made it down to Maryland to visit. That is reward enough.

Episode 60

Oh Samantha, Honey, Are You Sick?

Kids say the darndest things. And not only that, but as truthful as can be, unless they lie. (That has little to do with anything—I just wanted to say it.) Let me give you an example how truthful they can be: I was walking down a near empty mall. Coming toward me was a four- or five-year-old black child with his late-twenties father. As they passed me the young lad says, "Daddy, that man sure is ugly."

"Shh. Shh," and then to me, "I'm sorry."

"No need to be. He speaks openly! Have a good day, young man."

A few years before my time, a Basque first grader from Mountain Home was having a health lesson, when his teacher said, "You should never drink coffee because it will stunt your growth. We want to grow up big and strong."

"That's not true Mrs. Wilson. My mother drinks coffee all day long and she is as big as an elephant."

One of my grandson's teachers had a gerbil project in the first grade. During the time period the female gave birth to baby gerbils. She must have told the class that they had sex for that to happen. One of the teachers was very pregnant and Vince, in all innocence asked her, "Did you have sex to get that way?" The teacher sent him to the principal.

So onto my story about Samantha…

Samantha has waited patiently after school to see Mrs. Barayasarra.

"Mrs. Barayasarra. I'm feeling so sad."

"Oh Samantha, Honey, Are you sick?"

"No, we have to take our dog to the vet."

"Oh Honey, is your dog sick?"

"No, he has to have his balls cut off."

Mrs. Barayasarra ran out the door and into the classroom next to hers, leaving Samantha standing there. She related the story and both teachers were trying to control their laughter. As soon as she regained her composure, she went out to comfort Samantha. When she returned, Samantha had her hands on her hips and a frown on her face said, "It's not funny, Mrs. Barayasarra. You do know what balls are, don't you?

Episode 61

The Feelers Were Out

The meek shall inherit the earth

It was my brand new first day teaching at a brand new college in the state of Maryland. Well, maybe not quite that brand new: I taught my "brand newness" at Kuna High School in Idaho. After leaving the seminary, I received my B.S. degree in biology from the College of Idaho, January of 1958, and luck was with me as a rare opening for a science teacher opened up midyear. This can happen if the teacher there goes, well you know—he did. So anyway, after twelve and a half years of high school teaching, with Jan's encouragement and help, I returned to school for a Ph. D. in biology, was offered and accepted a teaching position at Chesapeake College in Wye Mills, Maryland.

It was the first day of school and I was excited if not a little anxious, as I left my efficiency Primrose apartment in Easton, turned right on Goldsborough Street and left on 50 and then a straight shot to Chesapeake College. Other than the dense fog, there was nothing unusual about the day, at least to me.

As I headed north on the dozen or so miles separating Easton from Wye Mills, I noticed a young black man hitchhiking. His backpack indicated that he may be a student—I *assumed* at Chesapeake. I passed him as I slowed down, pulled over and offered him a ride. He ran to catch up and entered the passenger side. He introduced himself, "Hi, I'm Martin Jenkins, I am a student at Chesapeake College. Are you going that way?"

"Hi, Martin. I'm a teacher there, and yes, I am going that way." A pleasant, friendly lad, I thought. Our paths will hopefully cross again someday.

"Did you see how close that car was to me as I pulled over? The fog's thick but . . . Is it often this bad around here?"

"Now and then. Most of the time schools open late ninety minutes. Hey! That's the second police car passing us! Something's happened big time at the 404 Junction—four-car—no six-car pileup. You know what that means?"

"No. What?"

"We. You and I. We had our feelers out."

"That one there passed me when I slowed down for you."

"And all six passed me by—you were the first to stop. Man."

"Martin, what did you mean by feelers being out?"

"It means that we are tuned into our physical and spiritual worlds and therefore things will go very nice for us." Then, pointing upward, "We are watched over."

"Because our feelers were out?"

We each adapted to life at academia: Martin as student, and me as an Associate Professor. The next semester, when Latif (Abdellatif Chafik) of Morocco was enrolled at Chesapeake College, our paths did indeed cross again. Latif was our son—except that he was not legally adopted. Technically, he was with us on a student visa. Since he was not a citizen, we received no help, that is to say he was NOT a foster child. I was not finished with work for the day, but he needed a ride home. We went to the student center to see if we could find someone going to Easton.

"Hey, are your feelers out? Hi, Martin."

"Hi, Bear. They sure are. What you need?"

"When are you headed home?"

"On my way now. Why?"

"Latif needs a ride home. Can he bum a ride off you?"

"No problem. Ready, Latif, let's go." And our paths crossed many times after that. Martin became like one of the family.

Episode 62
Cookbook

Not just any cookbook—a black, inch-thick, Betty Crocker cookbook, probably given to Victorina sometime in the forties so she could learn how to cook American—that is what this memory is about. Of course, she never used it, but she was proud of it. Daughter Felipa made cakes and pies, following the from-scratch recipes which make up the plot of this fine piece of literature. She made a topnotch coleslaw, which had to be unequaled in anyone's lifetime.

At times, I too tried my hand at cakes such as burnt sugar cake with burnt sugar frosting which was a challenge to make, or homemade donuts, which if one were poor enough, tasted good.

And they did taste good, made using lard in the dough and hot lard to fry them in.

The pages were brown and raggedy from age, frequent usage, being turned with greasy fingers, and gobs of dough which baptized pages here and there. As many pages were loose from the binding as were attached, but no pages were lost. The book had definitely entered book golden years and deserved some place of honor before going off to book heaven.

Felipa had no sentimental sense of attachment for anything. I have a shirt of my father's which has to be over eighty years old, which I retrieved from a pile of clothes she planned to take to a thrift store.

Felipa gave some of Mom's dresses and the cookbook to a Mexican wife of one of the men who worked for her daughter. The worker retired and he and his family returned to Mexico, taking the cookbook with them. A son later came back to the States as a barber. Felipa's daughter, Vickie, one day ran into Jesus and, in the short visit, the subject of the cookbook came up.

"You remember the cookbook your mother gave my mother? She so desperately wanted to learn English that she religiously read that book every day. Some of the words threw her and I laughed each time the pronounced tsp and tbsp. She never did accept that tsp and tbsp were the same as teaspoon and tablespoon. In Mexico, she taught all her friends recipes from that book. Needless to say, they all said tsp and tbsp the same as she did. She died last year but the cookbook is still with the family. I don't know what to do with it."

"Oh, I wish I had it," from Vickie. "It has so much sentimental value. My mom shouldn't have given it away, but . . . Just give it to a good home."

"I am going to Mexico for a month. What if I bring it back to you?"

"That is too much to ask."

"No problem!"

A few months go by. Vickie's phone rings. "That phone is driving me crazy. Hold on, I'm coming. Hello!"

"Vickie, Jesus here."

"Hola, Jesus. What can I do for you?"

"Can you meet me at Tapatia's? I need to see you."

"I can get away at 1:45. What is it about?"

"I can't tell you. See you at a quarter to two. *Adios.*"

"What can it be? Probably has three or four friends who need jobs."

She gets there at 1:30, goes in to get a table. When she gets inside, Jesus is already at a table.

"*Hola*, Jesus."

"*Hola*, Vickie." He rises, gives her a hug, and holds a chair for her to sit on. They order.

"I can't wait another second. Why did you need to see me?"

"I have something for you. Here, take this."

"What . . . The cookbook! *Gracias! Gracias! Gracias!* A miracle! A piece of my Amuma and my mother came back to me. Thank you, Jesus. *Gracias,* Jesus."

Episode 63
Agnes and Walter Cronkite

Hurricane Agnes hit the United States East Coast and it flooded in Olean, New York, some 400 miles inland, back in 1972. There was no tsunami or water surge, just steady rain for three days. The Allegheny River, running through Olean, overran the levies in a few places, which meant parts of the town flooded. Now, before we blame it all on the direct result of the hurricane, the Kinsua Dam on the Allegheny River, downstream from Olean, held back the water to keep Pittsburgh from flooding, and thus parts of Olean flooded. The reason being that the flooding of Pittsburgh would be more damaging than the flooding of smaller towns upstream.

"The river is really getting high," the last kid to check on it would update us, "It's flooding the road on the other side now." The other side had no dikes built along the river's banks.

"It's up to the windows of that row of houses across the river."

"It's up to the top of the doors of the houses."

"There is a trailer house floating down the river." That enticed the entire family and any other neighbors on the street to take a look. "Funny it didn't get caught sideways at the bridge and cause the river to go over at that point."

"It has reached past the first floor of the row of houses on the other side. Another twenty inches and we will get it here," one river checker would tell another, although both could see it for themselves.

"Portville is flooded; you can't drive down there," the other would return, though both heard the same newscast.

"No levies up there. Bet they wish they had some now."

"Well, it's a good thing for us they don't. If that water didn't spread out there, we would have more here and the river would be higher than it is."

That was the closest original observation of the discussions which took place. If one could forget the situation and its grave consequences, it was nice to see neighbors talking to one another. Tragic events seem to bring out the extremes in people—in some cases, the good as the friendly visiting or helping hands, but, in others, the not so good as looting in Portville. Two men were robbing the liquor store using a rowboat. Police, also in a boat, watched, letting the two load their boat and then moved in for the arrest. The reason given for the wait was so enough evidence was collected for the charges.

Rivers, such as the Allegheny, have somewhat regular patterns of flooding: every year certain areas flood; every few years, certain others flood; and every so many years, the river will experience a major flood as the 1972 one. In the case of the Allegheny, a major flood occurs every thirty years. True to schedule, the preceding major flooding was in 1942. Old timers, such as the next door neighbor, Ralph Schriver, were quick to tell you about the '42 flood.

"You should have been here in 1942. This street was under four feet of water and we had to stay on the second floor for a week until it was okay for us to clean out and use the lower floors. Of course, we took enough fresh water to last."

"Really?"

"Come on over. Let me show you. See that 'high water' mark on that wall? That's how high it got."

"The water is at the top of the dyke—about four more inches and our end of town floods," someone announces just before a patrol car drives up our street with a loud speaker, "You must evacuate this area immediately. The river is predicted to rise another foot before cresting in this area. You must evacuate this area immediately for higher ground. If you have no place to go, a shelter will be at the Olean High School gymnasium."

I received an invitation from Bill Penoyer, a fellow graduate student at St. Bonaventure University, for the family to stay with them, and Jan received a similar invitation from the Nixdorfs for our family to stay with them. We felt that there were too many of us to stay at either place, so we decided to split up: daughter Mary and I would stay with the Penoyers, and the rest of the family with the Nixdorfs. The Nixdorfs had two other families staying with them. Mary and I would not have added much burden after all.

Bill and I decided the next morning to walk to the river and see how high the water was near them. The river flowed just in front of Olean General Hospital. Several men were placing sandbags around the perimeter of the hospital in case the river overflowed at that location.

"Hey guys! Come and help us. Some of us have been here all night," cried a nearby volunteer.

"Oh, shit," I quietly said to Bill, "If I had expected to move sandbags, I wouldn't have worn these green and red plaid pants." Then to the one who invited us, "Sure, what can we do?"

To Bill, "Go around the hospital and bring that wheelbarrow here," and then, to me, "Take these sand bags from this pile to that barricade and place the bags as the others are doing."

Bill left for the wheelbarrow and I began carrying the full sandbags to where they needed to be placed. Carrying my first bag of sand, I noticed the television camera, a short distance away, facing my direction. "Oh, I will have to watch the news tonight to see if I'm on television," I thought to myself. Then, as I returned and picked up the next bag, the camera was focused right on me as I picked up the bag, carried it, and placed it in position. "I definitely will watch the news now. My green and red pants were probably the reason the cameras focused on me—the least likely type of person to work moving bags of sand."

For three days, the phones were dead in our area. I couldn't call my family in Idaho to let them know I was okay and they couldn't call me either. They were very concerned about me because national news carried Olean's flooding coast to coast. On the CBS News with Walter Cronkite, the news came on and my niece recognized me, "Hey, come quick, Uncle Jim's on television," and, sure enough, there I and my green and red pants were moving sandbags to keep the hospital from getting flooded.

The sad note to my fame, or notoriety, is that afterwards they didn't repeat being relieved that I was alive and well, but only, "where did you get those goddamn ugly—UGLY—green and red plaid pants?"

Episode 64

Agnes Revisited

Jump ahead to late December, 1972. Was the chapter concerning the flood of '72 closed? Not quite.

Just as in scary movies, when the dead monster has one more burst of fright left in him, so did Lady Agnes.

A troubled seventeen-year-old Olean, New York student was barricaded in the student counsel room on the third floor of Olean High School. He first shot and killed a school custodian who came to investigate an alarm . . . He then shot at random victims walking past the front of the school. Three bodies lay on the ground from his bullets. And anyone trying to reach them for help would face a barrage of bullets. National Guard tanks were brought in to shield ambulance staff trying to reach the bodies.

SWAT teams were trying to reach the lounge from inside the building with gas grenades. The sniper, equipped with gas masks, periodically shot down the hall at them. After a couple more victims, including a pregnant woman, the SWAT team hurled a gas grenade into the room, and lucky for them, his mask was defective. The shooting stopped and all was quiet when the sniper was captured unharmed.

The lad was so impressed how people came together during Hurricane Agnes flooding and helped one another during the crises, but a few months later this cooperation was gone. One explanation for his action was to create another reason for people to come together.

A short time after that the gunman took his own life in the Cattaraugus County Jail in Western New York State.

Let me connect this to Agnes. In the preceding episode, Agnes caught me in hideous red and green pants. This episode was a few months later, and much sadder: I knew of the gunman. My children went to school with him. The victims of his actions are in our thoughts and prayers as they should be but so is this young man, one of his victims.

An event such as the flooding of Olean, New York because of Hurricane Agnes brought out the best in some people and the worst in others. The young snipper was impressed with this aspect. He set about to create another crisis to get people to come together again. The gunman saw the uniting of people, even strangers because of the flooding. This was good. But a few months later, this good will was gone.

What if he could create a crisis to make people come together—that was his thought. He did what he did. A few days later, he took his own life. Although we may ask why, let us add him to the victims and pray for them all.

Episode 65

God Wants Him to Know

He is a Chicken Shit

Why did God create Judge Judy? Why did God create you? Why me? Maybe, he had in mind that each of us would contribute something to HIS overall plan. What if we don't do it; will there be a hole in the fabric of life? Or will someone else do it?

Why was I created? A very holy man told me that I may be doing God's work by letting some people know they are chicken shits. I know he was a holy man since, another time, he called me an asshole. Seriously, the Catholic priest who made the above remarks was indeed the holiest of all the priests I have ever known. He did not have to remind me that he was saved, Tuesday, the 14th at 10:24 a.m. He did not have that cheesy grin that many ministers have. In fact, when a socalled "born again" tells me they have been born again, I tend to notice how NOT born again they really are.

First, let me explain why he called me an asshole. I am an asshole, so perhaps he was just stating the obvious.

Actually, I had made a "Cursillo" and talked him into making one that I was going to be involved with. Without saying too much about what a Cursillo is, a type of retreat but not quite, or a weekend where one really lives their Christian faith.

It was lunch break and I was to give the first talk after lunch. Since I had a few minutes before we were to assemble, I was straightening out my sleeping area in the grade school multipurpose room. As I was putting my shaving soap in my dob kit, the dispense button was accidently pushed. I caught the gob of foaming soap in my right hand.

"Oh, shit, what do I do now?" Then I saw Father Willard walking by, "Hey, Father, I'm so nervous about my presentation; please wish me luck."

"Sure, Jimmy," as he put his left hand on my shoulder and extended his right hand to shake my hand. Perfect, he fell for it as I squished the shaving soap in his hand.

"You asshole!" he yelled as he chased me down the hall to rub the soap in my face.

The hall made a 90-degree turn just after the floor made a downward ramp. At the top of the ramp, I tried looking back to see how close Holy Mother Church was. Big mistake—I lost my footing and smashed, head first, into the cinder block wall. Had he killed me, I know he would have given me the last rites—not too many killers would do that, let me tell you. No-siree! He became a much closer friend after that, with All Saints Church across the street from Golden Leaf School, I saw him several times a week.

At the high school, a new student enrolled and during the first week, our boys began teasing him. I didn't want to step in since doing so would mean they would be even worse when I wasn't around. I went to the school counselor, Mark Roberts, and told him.

"Don't you know why?" He answers with a silly grin on his face.

"No, I don't."

"Go look at his permanent record."

I did and found a folder full of notes from his mother from grade one on up. "Please excuse Billy for his absence yesterday, he was sick," or something in that order. Then there it was, a note from the doctor who was attending as he was born: "I HAVE EXAMINED THIS PATIENT THOROUGHLY AND TO THE BEST OF MY ABILITY, I DECLARE THE INFANT TO BE A MALE."

A year of Physical Education was required of all students and this student needed it as much as the next. What was not necessary, was the shower that gym teachers required without exception. It is not only gay boys who looked at the weed-whackers of others—all did to see how they were compared to the others.

I went back to the office and he had the big grin which implied, "Now you know why they are picking on him!"

"You chicken shit," I said and walked away.

At the end of the day, I looked toward All Saints Church and there was Fr. Willard playing with his dog in the yard.

"Father, you got a minute?"

"Sure. Come on over," and when I got there, "What's the problem du jour?" I told him, sparing no details. We discussed the situation and what I could do for the kid.

Finally, I said, "I shouldn't have called him a chicken shit. Maybe I should apologize."

"Don't you dare apologize! He is a chicken shit and God wants him to know he is a chicken shit. God can't go around calling people chicken shits, so he uses people like you do to it."

Getting caught off guard and during the discussion after that, I knew this was indeed a holy man. I miss him so much. He is a retired Monsignor now—should have been a Bishop or Cardinal. I wonder why God didn't call on me to let people know that.

I do have a little problem with this explanation. One time in an argument with another person about a different matter, the person said I was "lower than whale shit." Was God using that person to let me know that? Were you, God?

Episode 66

Confession of a Soul

The departed dead we bury, but what do we do with the living dead? We shoot horses, don't we? We take our pets to the vet to be put to sleep, don't we? But what to do with our living dead relatives? We yell at them; we talk down to them; we avoid them; we patronize them; we pity them.

We do all expect to recall that in their day, they were the best teachers our children had; that they were fun to be with; that their opinions were sought out and followed; that they were handsome; that we counted on them for favors.

They loaned us money, which was never repaid. They helped us buy our farm which we eventually sold for a profit and yet, they will die penniless. They loaned us money to buy replacements for the worn tires on our cars, to pay monthly bills, so that we can take our families on vacation, and yet, they will die penniless. They helped us buy our homes, and yet, they will die homeless and penniless. They bought our numerous children savings bonds for Christmas and birthdays, and yet, they will die childless and penniless.

But there they are—the living dead. The living dead with their annoying mannerisms. They are ages behind the times, still living as if morals, values, and times are as they were when they went through puberty; before the impact of MTV—in fact, before the impact of television; before their values became irrelevant or at least not the same as they were when they were fifteen, giving the same advice to an eighty-one-year-old, no longer fourteen; a seventy-six-year-old, no longer nine, to a seventy-four-year-old, no longer seven, or a sixty-six-year-old, no longer two.

They babble, they drool, they fall, they mess in their Depends, and they let out spontaneous roars whether at home or in public, forgetting advice they gave a few years earlier, "You don't want to embarrass the family."

But now they have lived too long. They need help to bathe, to clothe. They need help to pee. Their once brilliant mind now slips in and out of reality, often not knowing which is real. Could I, or would I, pull the plug if one were there to pull? I think I might.

"But Lord, are You showing me that I fail caring for my lesser brother? Are You, Lord? Is that what is going on? Lord, I can give away possessions, as he did. I can die a pauper, as he did. But am I failing your test? Am I, Lord? Will, sorry, do, oh, Lord? Lord, do you allow do-overs?"

Episode 67
The Owl Just Won't Go Away
Part 1: The Sister I Never Knew: Alva

In Spanish folklore, seeing an owl near you on repeated nights is a forewarning of impending death of someone dear. A silly superstition? Maybe, but some version in various cultures exists and goes back to ancient Greeks—not a proof, I know. However, because of the frequent sightings in my family, I'm not going to rule it out. Should an owl appear to me, I will shit in my drawers, make an act of contrition, and hide under the bed.

First to leave this world was Alva who died the year before I was born. She was born at home with the umbilical wrapped around her neck causing brain damage. She had a vocabulary of one word which she used for everything, *moush*. All I remember of her is a very beautiful dead girl.

I've heard of another Basque family living in a house on our farm. They had a daughter a few years older than Alva who took a liking of Alva. Theresa and Alva played together. Theresa became ill one day, high temperature the second, and died the third. Alva followed her friend a day later. I see a beautiful heavenly story in the love of these two children, although one was handicapped, they both used their talents given by God to the fullest.

Episode 67
The Owl Just Won't Go Away
Part 2: The Telephone: Manuel

1946, September, Friday, 13: The day began in panic as the family hustled and bustled as it did on any school day. It was a normal daily panic—not especially bad, but certainly not especially good, either.

Victorina, Mom, was verbally prodding the children along. "*Arin! Arin! Jesus, Maria, eta Jose!* Can you move any slower, Felipa?" "What did you do with your other shoe, Frank? Felipa, help him find his shoe."

"Yes, I washed your Levis, Louis. You are not wearing unwashed pants four weeks in a row!"

"All the boys do, Mama. It's what they all do."

"And if they jump off the Grand View Bridge into the Snake River, does that mean you do it, too?"

"Ye ..."

"Don't get fresh with me. You are not! AND THAT'S THAT. May, San Antonio put it away!" Once St. Tony was invoked, it was best to accept defeat gracefully!

"Felipa, does Frank have his shoe? What is that out there in the yard? How in Jesus' name did that shoe get out there?"

"Jimmy, quit whining. I'm cooking the hot cakes as fast as I can. You'll get yours. Patience ..."

"Is there any more coffee?" Nemesio, Dad, asks, holding his cup out for a refill.

"My God! The older they get, the more like kids they get. Get your own damn coffee!"

"What brought that on? I just asked if there was any coffee left."
He received a glare as he filled his own cup.

Dad finished his fourth cup of coffee just as everyone was finally
ready. Louie, Felipa, Jimmy, and Frank climbed into the pickup, Felipa
up front with Dad and the three boys in back.

"Wait. Wait. Who is missing their lunch? Does everyone have all their
schoolwork?" Mom chased the pickup until it stopped and backed up.

Back at the house, Victorina used this quiet time to start the red
beans soaking for noon dinner and evening supper. Mike and Manuel
would sleep for another hour. This time, and during the later nap time,
she used to get most of her household chores done. One such job was
kneading the bread dough rising in a dishpan covered with a dishtowel.

"I'd better get to baking the bread, or I will have some very disappointed
children here shortly." She pinched the dough into loaves and smaller
biscuits.

The biscuits were ready just as the children arrived back home from
school. A fresh brewed pot of coffee was also ready, to go with the hot
buttered biscuits and apricot or green tomato jam.

Felipa poured herself a cup of coffee, set it on the table as she went
to get sugar and milk. In that split second, Manuel reached for the cup,
his soft baby hands grabbed the rim and pulled the hot coffee over
himself, over his face, his chest and down to the upper part of his legs.
Victorina grabbed a pitcher of cold water and quickly flushed Manuel's
body. She continued the cold water treatment until she was sure it was
not doing anything more for Manuel.

Victorina stayed up all night, trying to calm and comfort the irritable
and crying child. In the morning, the burns looked very nasty, so she
sent Frank and me to fetch Mrs. Spaulding, a retired registered nurse
who lived on the farm behind us.

Mrs. Spaulding said that Manuel should be seen by a doctor. There
was no doctor in Grand View and no telephones. The nearest doctor
was Dr. Lesser in Mountain Home, about twenty miles away.

Louie and Felipa were left in charge of the other children and the
farm as Dad, Mom, and I, interpreter for Mom, took Manuel to Dr.
Lesser.

"These are very severe burns. I want to keep him a day or two in our emergency clinic. It is staffed with nurses twenty-four hours. Two can stay overnight if you don't mind sleeping in easy chairs. Right now, I can give the child a shot to take care of the pain."

Nemesio had to return to the farm, so Victorina stayed with Manuel, and I stayed to translate for Mom. The next day Felipa was to replace me, bringing fresh clothing for Mom. Manuel, Mom, and I settled in the clinic. The nurse administered the shot which calmed Manuel. Manuel played games with me and giggled. It was almost as calming to Mom and me as it was to Manuel. It was indeed blessed relief to all—OR, was it the calm before the storm?

"Let's let the baby sleep, now. The shot makes him sleepy and he truly needs the rest. I'll have to repeat the shots every four hours to keep the pain in check," the nurse told us. Around four hours later, Manuel began getting irritable as predicted. The nurse took a vial from the cabinet and drew the medicine as before, wiped Manuel's bottom with an alcohol cotton ball and administered the injection. This time, Manuel emitted an ear piercing scream; his eyes rolled up and back so that they were ghostly white.

"Oh, my God! What have I done?" the nurse screamed. Then to me, "Call Dr. Lesser! Tell him to get here now! Oh, no! I used the wrong vial! Call the doctor, now!"

I ran to the telephone. I looked at it. I did not know how to use it. We did not have a phone. Grand View, in the entire town and surrounding valley, did not have a single phone. (Three years in the future, the town was to get one pay phone for the entire surrounding population of three hundred.) I stood there frozen—I did not know how to make a call—and my baby brother was dying.

"Pick up the receiver!" the nurse yelled at me.

I grabbed at the phone and what was the receiver came up, but I did not know what to do with it.

"Speak into it! Tell the operator, we need a doctor."

"Where? Where? How?" I cried.

Mom rushed into Manuel and held him to her bosom. The nurse came out, grabbed the phone from me and said, into the phone, "Operator.

This is an emergency! We need Dr. Lesser at the clinic immediately. This is life or death, operator!"

Dr. Lesser was there within minutes. Mom and I were asked to stay in the other room, while both doctor and nurse worked frantically with Manuel.

"My baby's dead! It's too late! My baby's dead! Maria, Mother of God! Oh, Jesus, Lord! My baby's dead!" Victorina was screaming, holding me tight, both to console me and to draw some strength from me.

"Mrs. Barayasarra, it was a tragic mistake. The second vial should not have been in the cabinet. When she reached for the vial she expected only the correct vial. Manuel is in a coma now. We can only hope and pray that his little body will come out of it. I'm so sorry. You may want to hold and sing to Manuel. And we will all pray."

But to no avail. Manuel died in his mother's arms the next day, Sunday, September 15, 1946.

That was the extent of my first telephone call. I said nothing, but that call very much changed several lives. Manuel was dead and I killed my brother.

Episode 67

The Owl Just Won't Go Away
Part 3: Father: Nemesio

Fast forward to 1958. When the owl, once again, visited the Barayasarra family. This time it was for Nemesio, born 1897, who died in 1958, six months shy of his sixty-first birthday. He survived the world pandemic flu which took the lives of many young Basque sheepherders. He had not seen a doctor since that time and had not attended church either, except to attend funerals.

The family had no health insurance around the time he died. I remember an office call was around 6:00 p.m. Dad was slightly cranky and we all did our best not to cross him. He had not been feeling well for a couple of days and we were debating to call the doctor anyway. In hindsight, I think he knew he was dying but kept it to himself.

I offered him a cough drop, out of character for me, and he accepted, out of character for him. When I recall that moment in my thoughts and prayers and the rare eye contact which occurred then, I am sure we were both sending out silent vibes to the other. Each of us wanted the acceptance and understanding from the other. How often I wish I had made the first move and hugged the man.

I was the son who never learned how to harness a horse, and thus failed the one true predictor whether or not I would ever be worth a goddamn. I also *was* the one who was told, "Kids now-a-days aren't worth a goddamn." And that my uterus will come out before he takes me anywhere again.

A few days before he died, I showed him my very first teaching contract from Kuna High School for $3,200.00 a year—very low in the United States. He even told me it was great. I often wondered if I raised my worth to the goddamn level in his opinion.

During my first semester, I took a night course from the College of Idaho. When I got home, Dad was sleeping in the living room which he has never done. Usually he complains about the lights or the noise. Again he knew he was dying and didn't want to be alone. At about 11:30, he jumped up, shouted, "This is it," ran across the room and fell. I caught him and for the first time in my life and the last moment of his, we embraced. Thank you God.

Episode 67
The Owl Just Won't Go Away
Part 4: Mother: Victorina

"I saw an owl last night, just outside my bedroom window."

"Sure, Mom."

"I did. I tell you, I saw the owl in the bushes just outside that window. Less than ten feet away."

"Okay! You saw an owl last night. They live out there."

"Yes, I know they live out there. But not right outside my window. Not in those bushes. All the years we lived here, there never were any owls there."

"So?"

"I have seen the owl for the last four or five days where no owl has been all the years we lived here. Do you see it? Look right there." I think she knew the legend of the owl. I think we either did not see any owls or if we saw any, we were not ready to act. Did the cock crow at our denial?

The ambulance took Victorina to the hospital. As she lay in the hospital bed, Nemesio appeared to her. "Do you see your dad?" she asked Felipa.

"No. Mom. I don't."

"He is standing right next to you in the doorway." She closed her eyes and left with Nemesio.

Episode 67
The Owl Just Won't Go Away
Part 5: Most Melancholy: Felipa

Felipa was the most melancholic of the bunch. It was easy to let her irritate you but that was the worst reaction to take: She wanted acceptance and love. The only girl growing up in a family of boys plus the anti-Basque atmosphere of the time in the area and the poverty of the family were factors she dealt with. She was bullied unmercifully.

Other than the gender aspect, the rest of the family had the same forces to deal with. Louie was a good athlete and that compensated greatly in the way he was treated. The remaining three graduated from Meridian where the difference was enormous.

Beside these factors she had two factors at home, not due to mistreatment but due to the perfectionism of family members. Victorina was a truly amazing person and therefore Felipa was always in Mom's shadow: Mom cooked better, Mom sewed better, and on down the line of comparisons. Except-except, her coleslaw was far better than Mom's. So were her cakes and pies.

And of course, she was always in Lou's shadow. Lou a type A person and the oldest was prone to give advice. Actually we all lived in his shadow.

Although she went through two short, failed marriages, she was blessed with a wonderful daughter who in turn was blessed with three sons who are my 'bombos. Phil, the world is much, much better because of you. A celestial hug to you.

Episode 67
The Owl Just Won't Go Away
Part 6: Modern Day Hermit: Louis

Louis J. Barayasarra, born February 7, 1929, died May 13, 2011, in a Caldwell nursing home. Lou was plagued with physical ailments for many, many years with complications from Crohn's, Parkinson's, high blood pressure, and two knees that had been grinding bone on bone for way too long. He was confined to a wheelchair for at least ten years. Unmarried, he had become used to getting his own way, way too dogmatic in his opinions. However, his mind was extremely active until the death of sister Felipa, four-and-a-half months earlier. His mind rapidly deteriorated during that short time. He died homeless, penniless, and family-less having given away everything he had to his siblings. He was very brilliant and generous as was his father.

Episode 67
The Owl Just Won't Go Away
Part 7: We Fought A Lot Frank

Frank was the fifth of Nemesio's immigrant family, and third son. He was named Frank after his father, Nemesio, who was called Frank because it was easier for the American to say.

In naming Lou, Dad suggested Bruno. He was named Luis. In naming me, Dad suggested Bruno. I was named Jaime. Frank was named Frank. Maybe he gave up on pushing for Bruno or maybe he liked the idea of a son named after him.

The owl sighting as a death predictor did not happen in Frank's case. Whether or not it is true, is not the point, but that the superstition is noted is—seriously or in jest.

In Frank's and my case one prediction, made over and over again, was made in frustration or as a habit but never ever as a prediction or a curse. In our fights, which were vicious, Mom was known to say, "*Jesus, Maria, eta Jose,*" or "It will be a miracle if one or both of you reach adulthood." Unless we accept a miracle, her prediction didn't happen. Frank was seventy-four at his death and I am eighty-two and alive, almost.

Now, one that did. A psychic predicted to me that Frank would at most have six months to live. He died five months after she made the prediction.

An unusual bit of information. I learned of Frank's death on Facebook, the day after he died. Does that mean he got in the last punch?

Episode 67
The Owl Just Won't Go Away
Part 8: Baraya Estates: Mike

Frank's death left the survivors of the first/second generation of the Nemesio immigrant family to Mike and myself. One positive result was it brought Mike and myself closer than we had ever been. In fact, not only Mike, but Cathy as well. A regular get-together event when we visited Idaho was to meet at the Golden Star Café for Spanish chow mein. Now that Mike is gone, I promise that we will continue this tradition and I will order "our" dish every time.

Mike was an excellent carpenter and a troubleshooter for mechanical problems. He was the only one who continued with farming and the only sibling who left this work with the recognition of having something named for him: *Baraya Estates*. It has a nice ring to it.

Death will be in thoughts as I recall my family members who are no longer with us. I see death as a step in our being. We all die. Hopefully we have improved what we have. I was there when Manuel received the wrong shot. I caught my dad when he ran across the room and died in my arms. I was with Lou when he died. And with Mike, when he was on a respiration machine, I spoke up first even though the thought was in everyone's mind.

Episode 67
The Owl Just Won't Go Away
Part 9: I Await the Owl

Death is an event in our human existence. It is as normal as birth, and although we can govern to an extent when it occurs, we cannot control whether or not it does. The sighting of the owl: is it a sinful non-Christian view? Or, perhaps it is a means of communing with us about life and death? For me, it is an interesting idea that is found in many cultures. I was impressed how much the owl was a part of my parents' culture. Nowhere have I suggested that my account is a typical Basque story: It is not. It is my observation of my parents and a story told in my way, but we happen to be proud Basques. At no time did I imply that my experience was better. Peeing in the stove is not a Basque thing, thank God: It was my thing. I chose to share it with you—and, my wife says I have no filter!

Whether an actual owl appears or doesn't to inform loved ones of my death does not alter the fact that I will die. If there is any truth to the idea, though the owl may alert us to get things in order.

In my account of Manuel's death, I did not relate the superstition of Friday the 13th. Manuel poured the coffee on himself on Friday the 13th, and he died on Sunday the 15th.

I am now the only person living of the first and second generation of the family of Nemesio and Victorina Barayasarra. I have lived the second-longest, besides my mother, who lived longer than me. The length of first and second generation ranks as follows: Manual, Alba, Nemesio, Frank,Mike, Felipa, Louis, Victorina,Jimmy. May Vickie, the "Half Wagon" survive a long earthly tenure as the best legacy Nemesio and Victorina left America.

Episode 68
I Can Pick Out My Own Bananas:
The Unfinished Musical

Shopping with Brother Lou was an event in itself. As a perfectionist and a mathematician, he was always aware of the best buys. Sister Phil (Felipa), the one to shop with him, was just the opposite and thus apt to grab the nearest item, regardless of price. As they passed the fruit, she reached for a bunch of bananas...

HOLD THAT THOUGHT!

Louie, a bachelor, and Felipa, after two failed marriages, lived together. Since they both needed someone else, the arrangement worked. As the next brother in the family, I often was amused with the two. Louie was the alpha male in our family and admittedly the most intelligent. Well, here we see two elderly people behaving, well, like *elderly people*. And yes I, too, am elderly. I was visiting one shopping day ... well, let's take a look at what happened.

"You ready Phil? Tell me what we need and I'll make a list."

Phil's first item. "Ten pounds of Idaho potatoes."

"You have three 10-pound sacks of potatoes over there. Unopened!" I pointed out.

"Oh but most of those are rotten," was her rebuttal.

"Ten pounds of Idaho potatoes," Lou started the list.

"Four loaves of white bread," said Phil.

"You have three-and-a-half loves from last time," again from me.

"But those are all dried out."

"But why buy so. . . ?"

"Four loaves of white bread," Lou interrupted as he added bread to the list.

"Three pounds of hamburger."

"Look," I say as I open the freezer door of the refrigerator, "it's full of hamburger—three pound packages."

"But it's all frozen and I need something quick for lunch."

"Three pounds of hamburger."

"Detergent, both kinds, dishes and clothes."

No comment from me. "Do you agree, Jim?" Lou asks me.

"WHAT? Oh sure both kinds—two Giant boxes of Tide and three Cascades."

"Two Tides."

"And three Cascades."

"And three Cascades."

"Two gallons of Mazola."

"You have an unopened gallon."

"It takes a lot of oil to fry peppers."

"Two gallons of Mazola on the list. How about peppers?"

"Oh yes, three pounds of big green peppers."

"And what are these?"

"Wrinkled."

"Lou did you get that? Peppers?"

"Three pounds of peppers—if fresh and large?"

And the list went on and on. "Thank you Jim for helping."

"It was my pleasure. It feels good when people listen to one."

BACK TO WHERE I SAID HOLD: Phil reaches for a bunch of bananas: "not those Phil. Get those over there, the greenish ones, those long greenish ones. Don't you know the long ones have more edible fruit per unit of skin. Those you are getting have less edible fruit per skin unit. DON'T YOU KNOW THAT?"

Then as if the heavens opened up, a lady shopper, doing a little soft shoe sings, "I believe the lady can—I said I believe the lady can—I BELIEVE THE LADY CAN—I BELIEVE THE LADY CAN, CAN PICK OUT HER GODDAMN BANANAS." The entire store sings as they march through the store. As the lady leads in marching and singing, the entire store joins in as Felipa is carried on shoulders of two young employees. Ends with Felipa belting out, "I CAN PICK OUT MY OWN BANANAS—I CAN PICK OUT MY OWN."

"Oh, I so enjoyed shopping today. Let's pick up a pizza for lunch, I can freeze the hamburger."

Appendix A

The following account was sent to me shortly after Latif was deported to Morocco.

To My Father
Say a few words on behalf of me
Should it be that you get there before I do
I'm hoping He will listen to what I have to say
But I'm sure without a doubt that He'll listen to you
No man no matter what religion He may be
Be it impossible to do what you have done
Adopting with all your mighty heart
An unwanted boy and making him your son
Treating him as if he were your own flesh and blood
You held him, loved him, and gave all you had
For a boy tormented from deep within
It was a miracle the day he found someone to call "Dad"
A father with a heart of gold
You were my savior as Jesus did it for us all
Unselfish and so loving every minute of my life
In my eyes you were and still are 100 feet tall
So thank you dad, or should I say dear old Dr. James
You grew grass in an abandoned wasted desert land
You gave me life and love that no one could ever have

And even in your olden days always held my hand

A father that any man could ever dream of

Dr. James P. Barayasarra, the man of the hour

When I was once a dying seed in the midst of them all

So thank you dad for making me a blooming flower

Love always, Latif

Appendix B

Abdellatif Chafik or Latif, as he was called, is our son, regardless of whether two governments say so or no. He has a fantastic story to tell, a story which involves three cultures playing a role. We talked about a joint venture but I expect my part to be introductions such as this or comments following his account.

A MAN WITHOUT A COUNTRY

...LIVING THE LIE...

Bewildered as someone quaintly uttered exceptionally!!! Little did they know, and never did I imagine the things which were to come. A little African boy who was born to a thirteen-year-old mother in a taxi in a land far away as they were going to the hospital would never have imagined that he would spend most of his life with a Basque family in a little quaint upstate New York town called Olean.

An invisible ache and an incurable pain within engulf my brittle bones as a cancer cell within the body. The soul of an unwanted child hides the secrets that only God the creator can remedy the hidden tortures within. Born to a country that was not mine and later to be deported from a country that I loved. So who am I? Am I Moroccan? Am I American? Or might I be Basque?

The middle-class Basque family—now mine—proud of their humble past have a story of their own to tell (*Seven Wagons and a Half*). If I can recall correctly after all I have gone through, the handsome young James and his princess Janet from Idaho decided, since their love of children overwhelmed them, while teaching in Nevada, to adopt a newly born little girl, whom they named Christina Marie. And as they say, God works in mysterious ways, and a few years later, Lisa Marie and Mary Ann were born to them. The decision to return to graduate school brought them to St. Bonaventure and Olean, where a little brown boy joined them, not as an infant but as a handsome young lad, all of eight years of age in a polyester suit which was not enough to hide my virtue from Allah, nor even from the Basque family I called *angelic*. To me this family was a gift from God, and in my later years kept me from going insane. To them I suppose it was an act of love as well. *I KNOW I WAS A GIFT FROM GOD TO THE FAMILY AS WELL—SOMETIMES LOVE HURTS.*

So how did it happen?

Appendix C

The following response by Dolores Totorica is reprinted with her permission.

JOSE FRANCISCO TOTORICAGUENA

By Dolores Totorica, responding to episode 42, "To the Doctor with Jose Totorica."

I read it and although I was just a few years old when he died, I have heard MANY stories about his laugh and what a bad driver he was . . . I want to send it on to my cousins—I am in the middle age range of thirty-nine first cousins . . . I just wrote a short bio of him for Koldo San Sebastián's book on Basque immigrants . . . TOTORICAGUENA URRIONABARRENECHEA, Jose Francisco. Born Dec. 15, 1878. Father was Juan Manuel Totoricaguena Mendiolea and mother Mª Josefa Dominga Urrionabarrenechea Fundasuri. Arrived to Nevada and Idaho about 1903. His first business partner was Jose "Bixar" Bengoechea. Also at another time, he was partners with Agapito Bideganeta. Three brothers quickly joined him in Owyhee. On Jun. 15, 1909, he married Leandra Erquiaga Foruria (native of Ispaster) in Mountain Home, ID. They had five children born in Owyhee County. The sheep business was good in those times, and Jose Francisco and his brothers, Diego, Julian, and Gregorio, at various times were partners. In 1917, he kept his holdings in real estate and livestock and returned to Euskadi (along with his brother Gregorio), and left his brother-in-law, Jose Domingo Erquiaga Foruria, in charge of the sheep operation.

However, after WWI, the bottom fell out of the wool and lamb prices. Erquiaga wrote to Jose Francisco and Gregorio to return, along with their sons, to keep the business afloat. There was no money to pay herders. Jose Francisco returned and brought his nephew, Pedro (native of Larraskitu), with him.

They arrived June 19, 1920. And in the following years, all the sons came to work for free and slowly rebuild the business. His brother Gregorio never returned and their differing perceptions of the business and money inputs and sharing caused a lifelong rift. Leandra and the girls returned in 1937 (after the bombing of Gernika) and Jose Francisco continued farming and ranching with his sons. He died in a car-train accident in Boise on Dec. 10, 1957.

Appendix D

CHESAPEAKE COLLEGE

May 28, 2002

Dr. James P. Barayasarra

Dear Jim:

While I knew you were planning to retire soon, it is hard to adjust to the news that you have made the decision. It will be difficult for me to think of Chesapeake College without Jim Barayasarra. You have been an exceptional teacher, and you have been an incredible advocate for our students and for minority students in particular.

More importantly, I think your project to document your family's history will be a great contribution and an inspiration to many who find themselves on the fringes of our society and culture. You were wrong on one point, however, and that was your comment about your own achievements. Your academic record and your extraordinary contributions as a teacher are successes by any standard. In fact, I would argue that your impact on society through your students is an achievement many would envy.

Jim, I wish you the best in your retirement and I look forward to reading *Seven Wagons and a Half* (*Zazpi Guridi eta Erdi*).

Sincerely

Stuart M. Bounds

President

Appendix E
The Drawings of Debora Camp

② Boy on Crate, watching hen Lay EGG!

③ Boy using lamb as a pillow.

④ "Joe Louis" eating NEW curtains

⑤ Ewe

⑥ Group

⑦ Lambs in field

Camp Wagon led by horses in Mountains

⑩ Campwagon with herder and dog under for cover.

⑪ Filthy Cowboy on Horseback w/cake. Mother between kids and Cowboy.

⑬ Man in Tub. Legs hanging outside.

⑬ Woman Dunking boy!

⑭ Man pushing Man in Wheelbarrow.

⑯ Coyote howling at moon.

20 Old Willow tree-Butchered Hogs hanging.

21 Border Collie sitting outside Camp Wagon / Night / Moon.

Made in the USA
Monee, IL
18 August 2020